D1113352

The Redeemer

Jack Kelley

WestBow
PRESS
A DIVISION OF THOMAS NELSON

WestBow Press books may be ordered through booksellers or by contacting:

WestBow Press
A Division of Thomas Nelson
1663 Liberty Drive
Bloomington, IN 47403
www.westbowpress.com
1-(866) 928-1240

Because of the dynamic nature of the Internet, any web addresses or
links contained in this book may have changed since publication and
may no longer be valid. The views expressed in this work are solely those
of the author and do not necessarily reflect the views of the publisher,
and the publisher hereby disclaims any responsibility for them.

Any people depicted in stock imagery provided by Thinkstock are models,
and such images are being used for illustrative purposes only.

Certain stock imagery © Thinkstock.

Unless otherwise indicated Bible quotations are taken from the NIV
version of the Bible. Copyright 1973, 1978, 1984 by Biblica, Inc.

ISBN: 978-1-4497-8242-9 (sc)
ISBN: 978-1-4497-8241-2 (e)

Library of Congress Control Number: 2013900972

Printed in the United States of America

WestBow Press rev. date: 1/16/2013

Dedication

This book is dedicated first and foremost to Our Lord Jesus by Whom and about Whom these prophecies are written, and second to my wife Samantha who has always been a loving and supporting helpmate, partner in ministry, and best friend.

About The Author

Before retiring into full time ministry, Jack Kelley was a successful management consultant with clients throughout the Western US and Canada. Since then he has devoted his time and energy to studying and teaching the Bible, and serving as teacher, counselor, and lay pastor. He has led several pilgrimages to Israel and Jordan, visiting New Testament sites in Turkey and Greece as well.

Jack is the author of Children's Stories Of The Bible, the Adult Version, 7 Things You Have To Know To Understand End Times Prophecy, and all the articles on gracethrufaith. com, the ministry's website. These articles and his answers to questions on the Bible are read thousands of times each day by pastors, teachers and students in over 190 countries and territories around the world and are regularly used as sermon topics, study guides, and sunday school lessons as well. This has made gracethrufaith.com one of the world's most popular Bible Study websites.

Jack and his family currently reside on the Baja Peninsula in Mexico where they also serve as volunteer missionaries in the local community.

Table of Contents

Introduction

Then I said, "Here I am, I have come – it is written about Me in the scroll" (**Psalm 40:7**)

Whether you're curious about inviting the Lord into your life, have recently done so and want to understand what it all means, or a long time believer who wants to reacquaint yourself with the basics of our faith, this book is for you. It's about what God intended in creating you, what has been stolen from you, and how God has been working since the dawn of time to get it back for you.

This book will give you a brief summary of the conditions and circumstances that led to man being in a state of permanent estrangement from God and then take you through a more detailed account of His incredible effort to bring us back to Him. We'll finish up with a summary of what He's doing for us now and what He's promised to do in the future. And as an added bonus we've included several short topical studies to further enhance your comprehension of God's word.

Reading this book won't substitute for good old

fashioned Bible study, but if you take the time to look up the references I've included in the text you'll find yourself becoming more comfortable using the Bible the next time you do undertake some personal study. You'll also be able to comply with the Apostle Paul's instruction to search the Scriptures to see if what I say is true (**Acts 17:11**). This is good advice for any Bible study you participate in.

From nearly 25 years of study I've come to the conclusion that there are three standards to apply when studying the Bible. Simply stated, I've learned to take a literal, historical, grammatical approach to interpreting what it says.

Literal means I believe the Bible is the inspired word of God to be taken at face value unless there is compelling reason to do otherwise (usually indicated in the context of the passage).

Historical means I place each passage in its proper historical setting, surrounded by the thoughts, attitudes and feelings prevalent at the time it was written to help me understand it better.

Grammatical means I use meanings of words that are consistent with their common understanding in the original language at the time of writing.

I believe this is the most accurate way to interpret the Bible. I also believe that even though the Bible consists of 66 "books" written by 40 different people over a period of about two thousand years, it's meant to be taken as a single message from God to man. The message is the man we call the Redeemer.

With that, let's begin The Story Of The Redeemer.

PART 1.
WHO STARTED THIS?

Chapter 1

The Redeemer Is Promised

And I will put enmity between you and the woman, and between your offspring and hers; he will crush your head, and you will strike his heel" (**Genesis 3:15**)

When God said, "Let there be light" and put the creation process in motion, He was making something designed to be perfect in every way. His crowning achievement was to create man and woman, immortal beings in His own image. He placed them in his perfect creation and told them to fill the earth with children, to subdue it and take dominion over every living thing (**Genesis 1:28**). So right from the beginning mankind was intended to rule planet Earth.

We don't know much about what Earth was like when God placed the first man and woman here because a whole lot has changed since then. But we do know that as God completed each step of the creation he called it good. And when He was finished He called it all very good **(Genesis 1:31).**

From little hints we find here and there in the Bible we can speculate that the weather was always perfect, the food was plentiful and free for the taking, and there was harmony between mankind and the animals. There were none of the disappointments, problems, or hardships you and I face on a daily basis. The Earth was literally a paradise where our first ancestors devoted themselves to exercising their creativity in a climate of perfect peace.

It might seem too good to be true, but it wasn't. At least not at the beginning. It was just like God intended it to be. But God has an enemy, someone we call Satan. His name comes from a Hebrew word that means adversary, and that's just what he is. He's against everything God is for and that includes us. Satan tricked our first parents into breaking the only rule God had given them, and when they did it brought devastating consequences to God's perfect creation.

The Bible calls violations of God's rules sins, and describes Adam and Eve's sin as eating forbidden fruit. It doesn't sound like much, but from the consequences it caused we can see that it must have been an extremely important thing to God.

It took a while for the full measure of those consequences to manifest themselves but within about 1650 years things had gotten so bad that the entire population of Earth had to be destroyed because of the sin Adam and Eve had introduced into the world. God sent a great flood and washed the Earth clean of all its sinful people. He saved only Noah and his family, eight people with whom He began again after the flood receded.

But we're getting ahead of ourselves. The first consequence of Adam and Eve's sin is they could no longer live in the Paradise God had created for them. Henceforth they would have to grow the food they ate and the concept of working for a living became part of the human condition. Additionally the creation would no longer cooperate with their efforts. Thorns and thistles began to grow, forerunners of the problems you and I face today in making a living. I believe sickness and disease began to appear at this time as well.

Also, Adam and Eve were no longer immortal but would have a finite lifespan. After the flood, successive generations experienced shorter and shorter lifespans until about 3,000 years ago when the average lifespan stabilized at about 70 years where it remains to this day (**Psalm 90:10**).

Therefore, just as sin entered the world through one man, and death through sin, and in this way death came to all men, because all sinned (**Romans 5:12**).

Another consequence was something scholars call a sin nature that was introduced into the human gene pool making it impossible for mankind to live in a manner pleasing to God. All of Adam and Eve's descendants became sinners by nature, unable to exist in the presence of God no matter how "good" they try to be. Since the Bible tells us the wages of sin is death, that means every human being ever born enters life destined to suffer eternal punishment for the sins they commit during their life.

At the same time God was announcing these consequences, He also promised to send a Redeemer who would defeat Satan and restore God's creation to the paradise it was intended to be. The dictionary defines a Redeemer as one charged with the duty of restoring the rights of another and avenging his wrongs.

In ancient times there was no organized legal system with law enforcement capabilities. Instead God gave man the law of redemption. If someone lost his property or was forced into slavery to work off his debts, his closest relative was responsible for redeeming him by paying off the debt for him. It was the only way someone could get his property or his freedom back. Also if someone was murdered, his close relative was required to chase down the murderer and take his life to avenge the murder.

It took a close relative to act as a either a Redeemer or avenger. Not just anyone could do it. This meant the Redeemer God promised to send would have to be a man.

Chapter 2

The Redeemer Awaits

For you know that it was not with perishable things such as silver or gold that you were redeemed from the empty way of life handed down to you from your forefathers, but with the precious blood of Christ, a lamb without blemish or defect. He was chosen before the creation of the world, but was revealed in these last times for your sake (**1 Peter 1:18-20**).

When Adam and Eve sinned, it was not a surprise to God. He knew it would happen before He created them and had already devised a plan for redeeming them. You may ask why He allowed this to happen, but it's important to realize that God created us with the ability and freedom to make our own choices. He doesn't control our behavior, but since He knows the end from the beginning He knows how we'll respond to circumstances that confront us before they happen. And He knows what the consequences of our choices will be. So before He created the world, He chose His son to be the Redeemer who would save us from our sins.

From the beginning it was understood that God's Redeemer would give His life in payment for the sins of mankind, thereby purchasing a full pardon for everyone who asked for it. Because the Redeemer would have to be a man to do do this, God's son had to become a man.

Because God created us with the ability to make our own choices He knew He would have to convince us of our need for a Redeemer. After all only Adam and Eve had experienced the creation before sin was introduced into it. No one else had first hand knowledge of the devastating changes caused by sin. This meant He would have to initiate a process of educating us. So God devised a series of circumstances designed to prove that without a Redeemer man is irretrievably lost.

The LORD saw how great man's wickedness on the earth had become, and that every inclination of the thoughts of his heart was only evil all the time (**Genesis 6:5**).

Between man's fall into sin and the Great Flood I spoke of earlier, God allowed man's conscience to govern his behavior without Divine interference. Because of the sin nature passed down from mankind's first parents, the result was a disaster and after a while the once perfect Creation became an evil place. The Lord was grieved by this and His heart was filled with pain. So He pronounced judgment upon the world and destroyed it by causing a world wide flood.

Then God blessed Noah and his sons, saying to them,"Be fruitful and increase in number and fill the earth" (**Genesis 9:1**).

After the flood God began again with Noah and his family, the only ones He had spared. He told them to go forth and replenish the Earth. But a couple of generations later Noah's descendants were still in the same location, having disobeyed God's commandment. Instead of spreading throughout the world they set about to build a great city and tower from which to study the stars (**Genesis 11:4**) and protect them selves in case God decided to send another flood.

To put an end to their disobedience God confused man's language according to their family groups. Being unable to communicate with each other, they stopped building the tower and moved away from each other, scattering themselves through out the world as God had intended all along (**Genesis 11:8-9**). But that didn't cure their rebellious nature and they drew away from God too, making false gods for themselves. God allowed this to go on for about 350 years after the flood before implementing the next phase of His plan.

"I will make you into a great nation and I will bless you; I will make your name great, and you will be a blessing. I will bless those who bless you, and whoever curses you I will curse; and all peoples on earth will be blessed through you" (**Genesis 12:2-3**)

God looked down from His throne and found Abraham, a man who had been looking for God. He promised Abraham great blessings that included a homeland for his descendants (**Genesis 17:8**) and a son for him and his wife Sarah, who had been unable to conceive (**Genesis 17:15-16**). But they grew tired of waiting and produced a son on their own through a surrogate wife. They named him Ishmael (**Genesis 16:1-2, Genesis 16:15**).

Later, Abraham and Sarah did have the son God promised and they named him Isaac. A few years after Isaac was born, they sent Ishmael and his mother away (**Genesis 21:8-13**) causing hostility between the descendants of Isaac (later called Jews) and the descendants of Ishmael (later called Arabs) that continues to this day.

Isaac grew up and had a son named Jacob. One day God visited Jacob and said He would fulfill the promises He had made to Abraham through him. To commemorate this God gave Jacob a new name, Israel. Israel had 12 sons whose descendants eventually became the 12 tribes of Israel and settled the land God had promised to Abraham.

But first God had to fulfill an obligation He had made to the people who were already living in the land. When He promised Abraham a homeland for his descendants He had given these people 400 years to repent and come back to Him. Since He knows the end from the beginning He knew they wouldn't do it when He promised their land to Abraham. But He had made a commitment to give them the time, so He sent Israel and his extended family to live in Egypt (**Genesis 15:13-16**). During their 400 years in Egypt they grew from a small group of 70 to a nation of well over a million people.

Now if you obey me fully and keep my covenant, then out of all nations you will be my treasured possession. Although the whole earth is mine, you will be for me a kingdom of priests and a holy nation.' These are the words you are to speak to the Israelites" (**Exodus 19:5-6**)

God had chosen the nation that would be called Israel to be the people through whom He would reveal His plan of redemption to the world. When He brought them out of Egypt about 2500 years had passed since the Creation. He used a man named Moses, a descendant of Israel's son Levi, to help Him. Moses had been adopted by Pharaoh's daughter and raised as a prince of Egypt, but he was the one God chose to lead His people to the land He promised to Abraham. On the way, He gave Moses the 10 Commandments and promised the Israelites a life of peace and plenty in a Kingdom of their own if they obeyed these 10 laws of His (**Exodus 19:5, Exodus 20:1-17**).

They promised to do so, but after receiving their homeland they experienced repeated periods of disobedience during which God used the surrounding nations to judge them. Although He had blessed the Israelites beyond any nation in the history of the world, they could not seem to consistently obey His laws, and every period of obedience was inevitably followed by times of rebellion against His law.

These things happened to them as examples and were written down as warnings for us, on whom the fulfillment of the ages has come (**1 Cor. 10:11**).

Of course God knew all this would happen from the beginning. He knew that fallen man could never live a sin free life, but He wanted man to learn this from his own experience. The reason He gave His people the 10 commandments was so they could evaluate their behavior against His law (**Romans 3:20**). That way they and all their descendants including us could realize that we can never live a good enough life to qualify for eternity with Him. Without a Redeemer we're hopelessly lost.

To help all the generations of mankind learn this lesson, God had a written record of the history of His interactions with man compiled. Earlier, He had chosen Moses to begin this monumental task and dictated to him all the important things that had happened in the previous 2500 years that were related to His plan of redemption. After that He appointed various men and women to keep the record updated and preserved intact.

I make known the end from the beginning, from ancient times, what is still to come (**Isaiah 46:10**).

So everyone could know this record was from Him, He also included things that hadn't happened yet. We call this prophecy. He did this so we could be sure the men and women who wrote it weren't just making things up. No humans can know the future unless God reveals it to them, so by including prophecy along with history, He was validating the book as His word. When the things He said would happen actually do happen, they prove that the book is true. There are thousands of prophecies scattered throughout the book. So many of them have already come to pass that it's impossible to deny His hand in writing it. It's the only so-called Holy Book that validates itself in this way, and it does so with 100% accuracy. In fact its accuracy is such that many think of prophecy as history written in advance.

We call this written record the Old Testament. It was written so you and I could learn about Him and learn from the mistakes mankind has made so we would know there is no circumstance or condition that will allow us to live an a manner pleasing to God. If he hadn't sent His Redeemer we would all perish.

Although the Redeemer would give His life at a specified time, His sacrifice would also apply to the past and the future, saving everyone who ever has or ever will ask in faith that his or her sins be forgiven. Accepting the Redeemer's once for all time sacrifice on our behalf makes it possible for God to see us as if we're as perfect as He is (**Hebrews 10:12-14**) and enables us to have the same intimate relationship with Him as Adam and Eve had before they sinned. It also restores our immortality so we can live forever with Him.

Chapter 3

The Redeemer is Given

The angel said to them, "Do not be afraid. I bring you good news of great joy that will be for all the people. Today in the town of David a Savior has been born to you; he is Christ the Lord. This will be a sign to you: You will find a baby wrapped in cloths and lying in a manger" (**Luke 2:10-12**).

Finally, 4000 years after the creation, the appointed time for the Redeemer arrived. We don't know why it was necessary for so much time to pass since sin had entered the world, because we won't know the full extent of God's purpose in creating us until we're with Him in eternity. What we do know is that He doesn't look at time the same way we do because the Bible says for Him a day is like a thousand years and a thousand years are like a day (**2 Peter 3:8**).

Through the prophets, God had told His people that when

the time came, the Redeemer would come as a baby boy (**Isaiah 9:6**). They said He would be born in Bethlehem (**Micah 5:2**), a little town in Israel near Jerusalem, to a young woman who was a virgin (**Isaiah 7:14**). Therefore He would have no biological father, but would be called the Son of God.

Furthermore they said He would not be born into a wealthy or prominent family and when He grew up there would be nothing in His outward appearance that would distinguish Him from others or cause them to be attracted to Him (**Isaiah 53:2**). For all intents and purposes, He would look like an ordinary man of ordinary means.

The angel said to her, "Do not be afraid, Mary, you have found favor with God. You will be with child and give birth to a son, and you are to give him the name Jesus. He will be great and will be called the Son of the Most High (**Luke 1:30-32**)

True to these prophecies, God chose a young woman named Mary to be the child's mother. She was a virgin, pledged to be married to a local man, a wood worker named Joseph. The angel Gabriel appeared to her and explained what was about to happen. By the power of the Holy Spirit she would become pregnant and give birth to the Son of God. Gabriel told her to name Him Jesus.

As we read the stories of His birth, we get the impression that it didn't seem to be much more than a minor local event. There was no great celebration of His arrival, nor even much of an awareness that it had taken place. Even the religious leaders, many of whom were familiar with the prophecies of His coming and actually saw them being fulfilled, seem to have ignored it. In fact only two small groups of people saw it for what it was.

And there were shepherds living out in the fields nearby, keeping watch over their flocks at night. An angel of the Lord appeared to them, and the glory of the Lord shone around them, and they were terrified. But the angel said to them, "Do not be afraid. I bring you good news of great joy that will be for all the people. Today in the town of David a Savior has been born to you; he is Christ the Lord (**Luke 2:8-11**).

First, there was a group of shepherds tending flocks of sheep outside Bethlehem. They knew what it was because an angel appeared to them and told them what had just happened.

This angel was joined by a heavenly choir praising God and proclaiming peace on Earth and good will toward men. The shepherds rushed to find the baby. He was in a manger in Bethlehem like the angel had told them. With Him were His mother Mary and Joseph, who had agreed to stay with Mary, take her as his wife, and raise the child as his own. Following Gabriel's instructions, they named the baby Jesus.

The shepherds told everyone they saw about this, and without fail the people were amazed, but there's no indication from the Bible that the celebration spread beyond the local area or even lasted for more than a day or two.

After Jesus was born in Bethlehem in Judea, during the time of

King Herod, Magi from the east came to Jerusalem and asked, "Where is the one who has been born king of the Jews? We saw his star in the east and have come to worship him" (**Matt. 2:1-2**)

The other group caused a somewhat bigger stir. They arrived in Jerusalem perhaps a year or two later, in a caravan that disturbed the whole city. The Bible calls them the Magi, or wise men.

They were priests from a near eastern nation called Parthia, a remnant of the once mighty Persian Empire, and were known far and wide for their influence in regional affairs. According to tradition, they were following a sign given to their forefathers by the prophet Daniel 500 years earlier, when Daniel was a trusted advisor to the Persian King Cyrus.

The sign was a star that would suddenly appear in the night sky. Daniel said the star would lead them to the one God had chosen to be Israel's ruler, and instructed them to hand this information down from father to son until the sign told them the time had come. Some even claim that the gifts of gold, frankincense, and myrrh that the Magi brought for the child had come from Daniel's own treasury.

"But you, Bethlehem Ephrathah, though you are small among the clans of Judah, out of you will come for me one who will be ruler over Israel, whose origins are from of old, from ancient times" (**Micah 5:2**)

So influential were the Magi that many considered them

17

to be kingmakers, and their endorsement was eagerly sought by those aspiring to rule. When they came to Jerusalem and inquired of King Herod as to the child's whereabouts, Herod appeared not to have heard about the Lord's birth, even though it probably happened a year or two previously. When he asked some of the chief priests where the Messiah was supposed to be born, they told him it was Bethlehem, based on their knowledge of **Micah 5:2**. But they also seemed unaware that this prophecy had been fulfilled.

Herod asked the Magi to let him know where they found the child. He wasn't even Jewish, but had been appointed to the throne because of his connections in Rome, and now these kingmakers were inquiring about the one who was born king of the Jews. Someone like that could legally challenge his right to rule. In his mind, he resolved to eliminate this potential rival as soon as possible.

But God thwarted his plans. He sent the Magi home by a different route to avoid passing through Jerusalem, and warned Joseph to flee into Egypt with Mary and Jesus and stay there until it was safe to return. Furious at being outwitted by the Magi and not realizing the family had fled, Herod gave orders to kill all the boys in Bethlehem who were two years old and under in an outrageous attempt to rid himself of this rival (**Matt. 2:1-18**).

With the child hidden in Egypt and the Magi back in Parthia things in Jerusalem soon returned to normal and the event that should have been cause for world wide celebration was forgotten.

Jesus remained in Egypt until Herod died after which God sent an angel to Joseph with a message that it was safe to come home. Joseph took his family back to Nazareth where Jesus lived until it was time to begin His ministry. By the time He had matured to adulthood hardly anyone remembered the special baby born in a manger in Bethlehem 30 years earlier.

Chapter 4

The Redeemer In Ministry

Leaving Nazareth, he went and lived in Capernaum, which was by the lake. From that time on Jesus began to preach, "Repent, for the kingdom of heaven is near" (**Matt. 4:13,17**)

According to **Luke 3:23** Jesus was about 30 years old when He began His ministry. When John the Baptist saw Him he said, *"Look, the Lamb of God who takes away the sin of the world"* (**John 1:29**) This was his way of saying, "Here's the Redeemer God promised us. He's going to sacrifice His life to pay for our sins."

Although He looked like an ordinary person, Jesus immediately distinguished Himself from ordinary men in two ways; what He said, and what He did.

"For God so loved the world that he gave his one and only Son,

that whoever believes in him shall not perish but have eternal life" (**John 3:16**).

What He said was so exciting to people that it came to be known as the Gospel, or Good News. He said the religious leaders had twisted and distorted God's Word into a religious system that was composed mainly of rules they made up. It was a misguided effort to make people behave in a way they thought was pleasing to God.

He said while God can't stand sin, there's no way anyone could ever behave in a manner pleasing to Him and that's why He sent His son. Believing in what God's Son would do on our behalf would give us something we could never achieve on our own, and that's eternal life. He said God hadn't sent Him into the world to condemn us for our sins, but to save us from the penalty of our sins (**John 3:16-17**).

He said we shouldn't worry about getting through life because God knows what we need before we do and will provide it for us. He said we should not try to get rich just so we could store up treasure on Earth but should focus on seeking God's Kingdom and His righteousness and let Him supply our needs. He said that by being concerned about what we could do for others instead of what we could get for ourselves we would be storing up treasure in Heaven, where it counts (**Matt. 6:19-34**).

This doesn't mean we're to live a life of sacrifice and deprivation, as some would have us believe, but that we should trust Him for our well being. He said He came so we could have life and have it abundantly (**John 10:10**).

The most important thing He said was that the only response His Father required of us was to believe in the one He sent (**John 6:28-29**). Over and over He stressed that we can never be "good" enough to meet God's standards, but if we just believe in Him and what He was doing for us we would have eternal life.

Then will the eyes of the blind be opened and the ears of the deaf unstopped. Then will the lame leap like a deer, and the mute tongue shout for joy (**Isaiah 35:5-6**).

What He did astonished people as well. He healed the sick, fed the poor, drove out demons, and even raised the dead. He calmed the storm and walked on water. He fulfilled hundreds of prophecies to confirm that He was the one God sent.

One time he was teaching a large crowd of mostly Jewish people who had gathered from all over. When He saw they were all getting hungry and there was no food for them He asked His disciples to collect whatever food they could find. They searched through the crowd and found only five small loaves of bread and two cooked fish. Offering a prayer to His father, He multiplied the bread and fish into enough food to feed all 5,000 men and probably at least that many women and children as well (**Matt. 14:31-21**). Another time He did the same with a crowd of over 4,000 Gentiles (**Mark 8:1-9**). These were meant to be examples of what He could do for us if we just trust Him to do it.

The Bible tells of several occasions when the first thing He did when a large crowd gathered to hear Him speak was to heal all their sick. News of this spread and soon people were bringing their sick from all around the area, even from neighboring countries, and He healed them all. And it wasn't just physical illness that He healed. The mentally ill received the same healing. And so did the blind and the crippled.

These were all things the Bible predicted the Redeemer would do, and He did them to show us that trusting in God and His promises to see to all our needs was real and it worked.

The point of this book is to show how Jesus saved us from our sins, redeemed us back from our slavery to sin, and restored our immortality. The four chapters you've just read have been a very general over view of the circumstances that led to His coming. Now we're going to get more specific in describing the most important events that have ever happened on Earth in a day-by-day account. We'll use the Jewish calendar for this to avoid confusing you about what happened and when, and the first day we'll look at was the 10th of Nisan in Israel, a day we know as Palm Sunday. Since the Jewish Sabbath is Saturday, Sunday is the first day of their week, and this particular Sunday was the day God chose to officially present the Redeemer to His people. Let's get started.

PART 2.
EIGHT DAYS THAT
CHANGED EVERYTHING

Chapter 5

The Redeemer In Victory

Palm Sunday, 10 Nisan

*Jesus took the Twelve aside and told them, "We are going up to
Jerusalem, and everything that is written by the prophets about the
Son of Man will be fulfilled. He will be handed over to the Gentiles.
They will mock him, insult him, spit on him, flog him and kill him.
On the third day he will rise again."* (**Luke 18:31–33**)

The time had come for the Redeemer to make His official
appearance in Jerusalem. Having spent the bulk of His
ministry in and around the Galilee, He now set His
sights on the Holy City for what He knew would be the
fulfillment of His mission to die for the sins of the people.
It was a long walk and would require most of the day.

*Rejoice greatly, O Daughter of Zion! Shout, Daughter of
Jerusalem! See, your king comes to you, righteous and having*

salvation, gentle and riding on a donkey, on a colt, the foal of a donkey (**Zechariah 9:9**)

As they came to the twin villages of Bethpage and Bethany on the eastern slope of the Mt. Of Olives, Jesus sent two disciples ahead to fetch the donkey He knew would be waiting there, and as He crested the Mt. Of Olives he saw the beautiful city spread before Him. Large crowds were arriving for the Passover and many of them had already heard that He had recently raised Lazarus from the grave (**John 11:1-44**). Surely this was the long awaited Redeemer. Some spread their cloaks on the road while others cut palm branches and laid them in front of Him as He rode down the western slope, across the Kidron valley, and into the city. There were large joyful crowds both in front of and behind Him spontaneously shouting the portion of **Psalm 118** that was reserved for the entrance of the Messiah into the city.

"Hosanna! Blessed is he who comes in the name of the Lord! Blessed is the coming kingdom of our father David! Hosanna in the highest!" (**Mark 11:9-10**)

A contingent of the ever present Pharisees was there, and some of them instructed Jesus to rebuke His followers. If Jesus was not the promised Redeemer, and they didn't think He was, the crowds were committing blasphemy.

"I tell you," He replied, *"If they keep quiet the stones will cry out."* (**Luke 19:40**)

It was 483 years from the day Persian King Artaxerxes had

issued the decree authorizing the Jews to rebuild Jerusalem after the 70 year Babylonian captivity (**Nehemiah 2:1-10**). It was the day ordained in history for the Redeemer to officially present Himself to Israel (**Daniel 9:25**), and instead of rebuking His disciples He rebuked the Pharisees for not knowing this.

As he approached Jerusalem and saw the city, he wept over it and said, "If you, even you, had only known on this day what would bring you peace—but now it is hidden from your eyes. The days will come upon you when your enemies will build an embankment against you and encircle you and hem you in on every side. They will dash you to the ground, you and the children within your walls. They will not leave one stone on another, because you did not recognize the time of God's coming to you." (**Luke 19:41-44**)

It was also the 10th day of Nisan, the day when God commanded the Jews to select the Passover lamb. Then for three days they were to carefully inspect it to make sure it had no spot or blemish that would prevent it from being used in the Passover celebration on the 14th. (**Exodus 12:3,6**). Over the next three days Jesus would be subjected to the most intense scrutiny of His ministry as the Jewish leadership tried to find some error in His teaching that they could use to discredit Him.

Matthew and Luke take us right into their accounts of the Temple clearing, causing some to believe that it might have happened on that first Palm Sunday. But Mark makes it clear that when Jesus finally entered Jerusalem He went to the Temple and looked around at everything, but since it was late He took the disciples and went back to Bethany where they were staying (**Mark 11:11**).

Clearing The Temple. Monday 11 Nisan

In the morning Jesus left Bethany in the company of His disciples. He was hungry and seeing a fig tree went to pick some its fruit, but there was none. He cursed the tree saying, *"May no one ever eat fruit from you again"* (**Mark 11:14**). Much has been made of this, the only negative miracle Jesus ever performed. Some scholars see it as a prophecy that Israel would soon wither and die, never again bearing fruit for the Kingdom. History has given evidence supporting the validity of their interpretation.

Upon reaching Jerusalem, the Lord headed straight for the Temple and when He got there He began driving out those who were buying and selling, overturning the tables of the money changers. He said to them, *"It is written, My house will be called a house of prayer* (**Isaiah 56:7**), *but you have turned it into a den of robbers* (**Jere. 7:11**)."

He was referring to the fact that the pilgrims who traveled a great distance found it safer to buy animals for their sacrifices in Jerusalem than try and bring them from home. The priests would only accept Temple coinage in payment for these animals and for offerings the people made. Some say they charged exorbitant prices for the animals and also maintained an unfavorable exchange rate for foreign currency. Most likely, this is what prompted the Lord's accusation.

Word that Jesus was at the Temple spread quickly. The blind and lame came to Him and He healed them. The children who had also gathered around began shouting, "Hosanna to the Son of David", a Messianic reference. The chief priests and teachers of the Law were indignant but Jesus said, *"Have you never read, 'From the lips of children and infants you have ordained praise'* (**Psalm 8:2**)? Then He left the city and returned to Bethany. (**Matt. 21:14-17**)

A Long Day Of Teaching And Confrontation. Tuesday 12 Nisan

The next morning Jesus set out early for the Temple. After being challenged by the Pharisees again, He launched into a series of parables. A parable is a fictional story placed in an Earthly context that's designed to convey a Heavenly truth. Every character or event is symbolic of something else. Understanding what they symbolize helps us discover the Heavenly truth.

He began with the parable of the 2 sons, one obedient and other not. One son said he would obey then didn't. He represents the Pharisees. The other son said he would not obey but then did. He represents the tax collectors and prostitutes. Jesus said to the Pharisees, *"I tell you the truth, the tax collectors and the prostitutes are entering the kingdom of God ahead of you. For John came to you to show you the way of righteousness, and you did not believe him, but the tax collectors and the prostitutes did. And even after you saw this, you did not repent and believe him"* (**Matt. 21:28-32**).

Then came the Parable of the Tenants. It's about a landowner (God) who rented his vineyard (His Land) to tenants (Israel). But when harvest time came they refused to give him his share of the fruit (the salvation of mankind). They killed the servants he sent (prophets) and even killed his son (Jesus) in an effort to keep everything for themselves.

Jesus asked them what they thought the landowner should do to them when he returns. They said he should bring them to a wretched end and rent his vineyard to other tenants who will give him his share. Jesus agreed and said, *"Therefore I tell you that the kingdom of God will be taken away from you and given to a people who will produce its fruit"*

The chief priests and Pharisees understood that Jesus was talking about them (**Matt. 21:33-46**).

In the Parable of the Wedding Banquet, which came next, Jesus spoke of the invited guests refusing to attend a banquet celebrating the marriage of a king's son. The banquet represents the Kingdom of God, the King is God, His Son is Jesus, and the invited guests are Israel. Enraged at their refusal to attend his banquet, the king sent his army and burned their city (Jerusalem). Then, as the time for the banquet approached he sent his servants to collect anyone they could find to attend as his guests. As the king entered the banquet, He found a guest without a wedding garment and had him ejected. (**Matt. 22:1-14**)

Many Christians have misinterpreted the group of guests as representing the Church. But the Church is the bride (**2 Cor. 11:2**) not a random group of last minute guests. Who then are the guests and who is the one ejected from the wedding?

Isaiah 61:10 tells us when we become believers the Lord arrays us in a garment of salvation, a robe of righteousness. It's imputed to us by faith (**Romans 3:21-22**), not by works. In the parable, the wedding garment stands for this righteousness.

The last minute guests are known as Tribulation survivors, people who will live through the End Times judgments that will come upon the whole world to prepare it for the coming Kingdom of God. During these judgments some will become believers while others won't. The guest who is ejected from the banquet symbolizes these unbelievers seeking to enter the Kingdom without being clothed in the Lord's garment of salvation.

At the time of the 2nd Coming Jesus will gather all Tribulation survivors together. Believers will be welcomed into the Kingdom, while unbelievers will be escorted off the planet to eternal punishment.

In an effort to trap Him, the Pharisees asked Him if it was right to pay taxes to Caesar. Responding with a question of His own, Jesus took a coin and asked them whose portrait and inscription were on the coin. When they said it was Caesar's Jesus said, *"Give to Caesar what is Caesar's and to God what is God's".* In other words, He told them to pay their taxes as the government required, but since their life belongs to God they should give that to Him. They were amazed at His answers so they left Him and went away (**Matt. 22:15-22**).

Then another group, Sadducees this time, asked Jesus about marriage in the resurrection. Sadducees didn't believe in an actual resurrection but told Jesus a story of a woman who sequentially married seven brothers, each marriage following the death of the preceding brother. It was an outlandish exaggeration of the law of leverite marriage, which provided for the brother of an Israelite who dies without an heir to marry his brother's widow and have a child with her to produce an heir for the dead brother's inheritance (**Deut. 25:5-6**).

Jesus accused them of not knowing the Scriptures or the power of God. In the resurrection there will be no marriage. Then He attacked their denial of the resurrection. He reminded them that in the Book of Moses (the Torah) God called Himself the God of Abraham, Isaac, and Jacob. *"He is not the God of the dead but of the Living,"* He said. The people listening were astonished at His answers (**Matt. 22:23-33**)

Then they asked Him which of the commandments is the most important. He replied, quoting **Deut. 6:5** and **Lev. 19:18**. *"Love the Lord your God with all your heart and with all your soul and with all your mind. This is the first and greatest commandment. And the second is like it: Love your neighbor as yourself. All the Law and the Prophets hang on these two commandments."* (**Matt. 22:37-40**)

The first 4 commandments explain how we are to love the Lord, and the last 6 tell us how to love one another. Together they summarize all of God's word.

Then He asked the Pharisees a question.

"What do you think about the Christ? Whose son is he?"

"The son of David," they replied.

He said to them, "How is it then that David, speaking by the Spirit, calls him 'Lord'? For he says,

"'The LORD said to my Lord: "Sit at my right hand until I put your enemies under your feet"' (**Psalm 110:1**)

If then David calls him 'Lord,' how can he be his son?" No one could say a word in reply, and from that day on no one dared to ask him any more questions. (**Matt. 22:42–46**)

His point was that Lord is a title used to address a superior. Since a son is not superior to his father David would not call his son Lord. That means while Jesus was biologically a descendant of David's through his mother Mary, He was also the Son of God and therefore superior to David. His examination was complete. They had found no fault in Him. He was qualified to be the Passover Lamb.

Now It's My Turn

Having defended Himself against all their tricks and traps, the Lord now went on the offensive with a scathing indictment of their religious practices. It was pay back time for all the resistance they'd shown, all the criticism they'd leveled at him. He called them hypocrites and told the people to obey what they say but not to do what they do. He said all their actions are just for show to make themselves look pious and important. Not only would they not enter the Kingdom, but they prevented others from entering as well. He called them false teachers and blind guides, saying they were obsessed with little things but neglected the more important matters of the Law. He said they were like white washed tombs, all clean on the outside but full of dead men's bones and everything unclean. He called them snakes, a brood of vipers (seed of the serpent) and held them responsible for the blood of all the prophets their predecessors had killed (**Matt. 23:1-36**).

"O Jerusalem, Jerusalem," He cried, "You who kill the prophets and stone those sent to you, how often I have longed to gather your children together, as a hen gathers her chicks under her wings, but you were not willing. Look, your house is left to you desolate. For I tell you, you will not see me again until you say, 'Blessed is he who comes in the name of the Lord.'" (**Matt. 23:37-39**)

Then He left the Temple and walked out of the city. But His day was not over. On the way back to Bethany the Lord gave 4 of His disciples a critical lesson on End Times prophecy.

A Prophecy Lesson. Tuesday 12 Nisan (Cont'd)

Jesus left the temple and was walking away when his disciples came up to him to call his attention to its buildings. "Do you see all these things?" he asked. "I tell you the truth, not one stone here will be left on another; every one will be thrown down." (**Matt. 24:1-2**)

How this must have astonished the disciples. Over 500 years earlier the prophet Daniel had revealed that beginning with a decree authorizing the reconstruction of Jerusalem, which had lain in ruins for 70 years, Israel would be given 490 years during which all necessary preparations for the Messianic Kingdom would be made. They would finish transgression, put an end to sin, atone for wickedness, bring in everlasting righteousness, seal up vision and prophecy, and anoint the most holy (place). The most holy place refers to the Temple. Accomplishing this would require the Redeemer to come and die for the sins of the people (**Daniel 9:24-26**).

The disciples knew the 483 year mark had been reached a few days earlier and that the Redeemer, Jesus, was among them. He had explained to them that when they got to Jerusalem He would be executed but would come back from the grave three days later (**Matt. 16:21, Luke 18:31-33**). So there were only seven years left of the 490 years. The Temple had been undergoing a major reconstruction that so far had required 46 years (**John 2:20**) and wasn't complete yet. But now Jesus was saying everything would be torn down. Not one stone would be left standing on another. How could that be?

As they began their trek up the Mt. of Olives on their way back to Bethany, four of the disciples (Peter, James, John and Andrew) approached Jesus to ask Him about these things. They had 3 questions for Him. First they wanted to know when this would happen. They also wanted to know what would be the sign of His coming, and what would be the sign of the end of the age (**Matt. 24:3**).

By their questions we can tell they'd been discussing this among themselves. Wanting to know when the Temple would be destroyed was an obvious reaction to his earlier statement, but the Lord's 2nd Coming was still a new idea to them. And if the Temple was going to be torn down how would they know when the end of the age would come? They certainly could no longer count on it it happening in 7 years.

Matthew's account of the Lord's response does not contain an answer to their first question. But Luke's does, so let's go there first.

Jesus told them, *"When you see Jerusalem being surrounded by armies you will know its desolation is near. There will be great distress in the land (Israel) and wrath against this people (the Jews). They will fall by the sword and be taken as prisoners to all the nations. Jerusalem will be trampled on by the Gentiles until the times of the Gentiles are fulfilled"* (**Luke 21:20, 23,24**).

The disciples were to understand that when they saw the Roman Armies surrounding Jerusalem it would mean the Temple was about to be destroyed. This began to happen about 33 years later. It started when the Jews mounted an unsuccessful revolt against Rome in 66 AD. The Romans responded by laying siege to Jerusalem and by 70AD Jerusalem and the Temple lay in ruins. And from that day to the persent Jesrusalem has been subjected to a continuous struggle for control by just about every world power that came along.

In answering their 2nd and 3rd questions, Jesus began with an overview. In the times ahead there would be false messiahs, wars, and rumors of wars, but they would not signal the end. He said nation would rise against nation and kingdom against kingdom. There would be famines and earthquakes in various places. He characterized these as the beginning of birth pangs, meaning they would be signals that the time of the 2nd Coming was approaching like labor pains tell a pregnant woman the time of her baby's birth is approaching. As they became more frequent and more intense it would mean the time was coming closer and closer.

He said the Jewish people would be persecuted and hated by all nations because they would be blamed for His death. There would be false prophets, and an increase of wickedness, but he who stands firm to the end would be saved (**Matt. 24:4-13**). He completed His overview by saying the Gospel would be preached in the whole world as a testimony to all nations, and then the end will come (**Matt. 24:14**).

Then the Lord gave them the first specific sign in answer to their questions. He said when the people of Judea see the abomination that causes desolation standing in the

Holy Place they should immediately flee for their lives (**Matt. 24:15-16**).

The term abomination that causes desolation was well known to them even though it had only happened once previously. About 200 years earlier the Syrian ruler Antiochus Epiphanes had captured the Temple and placed an image of the Greek god Zeus with his own face on it there and demanded that the people worship it on pain of death. This rendered the Temple unfit for use and started the three and one half year long Maccabean revolt. The annual celebration of their victory over the Syrians is called the Feast of Hanukkah and is still observed today. Every Jew knows the meaning of the abomination of desolation from this celebration. It's a sign they will all recognize.

Jesus told the people of Judea to pray their flight wouldn't be in winter or on a Sabbath when that happens again because it would signal the beginning of the Great Tribulation, a time of judgment more severe than anything that's ever happened on Earth (**Matt. 24:21**). It's more difficult to flee to a safe place in the winter and it's against their Law for Jews to travel on the Sabbath.

It's hard to over estimate the significance of that statement. Even though Jesus had earlier warned the disciples the Temple was soon to be destroyed, He now said the Jewish nation would have a working Temple again as the End of the Age approached. From about 135 AD until 1948 there was no Jewish nation, and since 70AD there hasn't been a Temple there.

With 20-20 hindsight we can see that with the rejection of the Redeemer, Daniel's 70 week prophecy was suspended 7 years short of it's fulfillment. 20 years later, the Lord's brother James explained to the early Church leaders that this suspension would remain in force while the Lord took from the Gentiles a people for Himself (the Church) and after that Israel would be restored (**Acts 15:13-18**). Therefore the Church Age didn't cancel the remaining seven years of Daniel's prophecy, it has just postponed their fulfillment. After the Church Age ends Israel's final 7 years will resume and this time all their objectives will be reached.

It's important to understand that Jesus hasn't been talking about the Church in this discussion at all. In the first place, our salvation is not contingent upon standing firm to the end. Our salvation was assured from the moment we believed (**Ephes. 1:13-14**). God has set His seal of ownership on us and put His Spirit in our hearts as a deposit, guaranteeing our eternal life with Him (**2 Cor. 1:21-22**).

Second, we don't live in Judea, which is the name by which Israel was known in the Lord's time. And third, there's no Sabbath travel restriction for us like there is for the Jewish people.

Before these last seven years begin, Jesus will gather His Church from the earth and take us to be with Him in Heaven. It's an event called the rapture of the Church in which every believer alive at the time will suddenly disappear without a trace (**1 Cor. 15:51-52, 1 Thes. 4:16-17**). At that point the Church Age will abruptly end. People will still become believers after this, but they won't be part of the Church.

That's why there's no mention of the Church anywhere in this discussion. Jesus was a speaking as a Jewish prophet explaining to His Jewish disciples about the end times as they concern the Jewish people. Remember, their questions to Him were about the remaining seven years of Daniel's 70 Week prophecy, which is all about Israel.

The Great Tribulation that begins with the abomination that causes desolation will be the last half of this 7 year period and as I said, it will be the worst time the world has ever seen or ever will see again . It's purpose will be to discipline Israel in preparation for the coming Kingdom and completely destroy the unbelieving nations of the world to which the Jews have been scattered (**Jeremiah 30:1-11**). No period of time is more carefully measured in all the Bible. It's variously described as being 3 ½ years, or 42 months or 1260 days long. Jesus called it the Great Tribulation. He said if it was allowed it to run its course not a single human being would survive, but for the sake of His elect He will put an end to it at its appointed time (**Matt. 24:22**).

Immediately after the end of the Great Tribulation the Sun and Moon will go dark and the stars will fall from the sky. The world will be plunged into darkness. At that time the sign of the Son of Man (Jesus) will appear as the only light in the sky and all the nations of the Earth will mourn. Then they will see Him coming on the clouds of the sky with power and great glory (**Matt. 24:29-30**).

Jesus said in effect that the generation of people being born when the first of the end times signs appear will still be alive at the 2nd Coming (**Matt. 24:34**). Since He began by saying there will be a nation of Jewish people in the Promised Land at the End times, and since that hadn't been the case until 1948, many scholars believe that the rebirth of Israel was the event that kicked off the End Times. If so, then many of the people who were born in 1948 will still be alive when He returns.

"No one knows about that day or hour, not even the angels in heaven, nor the Son, but only the Father" (**Matt. 24:36**)

From **Matt. 24:29-30** we can tell that Jesus was speaking about the day and hour of his return to Earth after the end of the Great Tribulation, and while you may have seen different different interpretations of what follows, it's important for you to understand that all of it pertains to the time immediately surrounding the 2nd Coming.

First He said it would be similar to the days of Noah. Before the flood unbelievers had no idea what was coming and why, and when Noah tried to warn them about it they just laughed, as if he was crazy. Right up to the day of the flood, they kept on going about their lives, clueless to the fact that life as they knew it was about to end forever. It will be like that at the End of the Age as well. This is why Jesus said the nations will mourn when they see Him coming (**Matt.24:30**). They'll finally realize that what they've been hearing is true and it will be too late for them to do anything in response.

He gave three examples where two people appear to be just alike and are doing the same things, but one would be received into the Kingdom while the other would be sent away to eternal punishment. Matthew mentioned only two of them, the men in the field and the women grinding with a hand mill (**Matt. 24:40-41**). Luke added the two people sleeping in the same bed (**Luke 17:34**). The Lord's point was that what differentiated them was not external and physical, but was internal and spiritual. It's what they believe that makes them different.

The key to understanding these examples lies in the words taken and left in **Matt. 24:40-41**. The Greek word for taken means to take unto oneself, or receive, and refers to surviving believers who will be received into the Kingdom. The word for left means to send away. These are the unbelievers who will be sent away for judgment. He was speaking of Tribulation survivors who will stand before the Lord upon His return to learn of their destiny.

Then He gave a warning that those who survive the Great Tribulation will not know the day or hour of His return so they should be watching for Him like a homeowner watches for a thief he knows is coming (**Matt. 24:42-44**).

Next, the Lord told them four parables, each one an

example of how it will be just after the 2nd Coming. Once again there's been no mention of a rapture or even of the Church itself. Nor will there be. This discussion is about Israel's last seven years. The Church will be gone by then.

The Faithful Servant. (Matt. 24:45-51)

The first parable is about servants of a master's house who've been given the responsibility of seeing that his other servants are fed . Remember, a parable is a fictional story placed in an Earthly context that's designed to convey a Heavenly truth. Every character or event is symbolic of something else. Understanding what they symbolize helps us discover the Heavenly truth.

The servants in charge are post rapture ministers of the Gospel, which is symbolized by the food they provide for the other servants, their congregations. Their master is the Lord. They won't know exactly when He will return but when He does those who have been faithfully preaching the Gospel of the Kingdom will be rewarded. Those who've misled their flocks and preached a false Gospel will be punished. James warned us that those who teach will be judged more strictly (**James 3:1**). By their actions, these servants will have shown themselves to be false teachers and will be judged accordingly.

Keep in mind that eternal security is a blessing given only to the Church. If you're a believer your inheritance has been guaranteed by God (**Ephesians 1:13-14**). You will spend eternity with Him and no power in Heaven or on Earth can ever change that. But those who become believers after the rapture of the Church will have to maintain their own righteousness or risk losing their salvation. **Rev. 14:12** says they'll have to keep God's commandments and remain faithful to Jesus. And **Rev. 16:15** says, *"Behold I come Like a thief. Blessed is he who stays awake and keeps his clothes with him so that he may not go naked and be shamefully exposed."* And remember, when used symbolically, clothing stands for righteousness (**Isaiah 61:10**) and post rapture believers will be responsible for their own.

The Ten Virgins. (Matt. 25:1-13)

Next He told the parable of the 10 virgins or bridesmaids. Once again He began by identifying the time frame of the parable. By saying "at that time" He was referring to **Matt. 24:36,** the day and hour of His 2nd Coming, which follows the end of the Great Tribulation (**Matt. 24:29**).

The story is about 10 young women who've been waiting a long time for the bridegroom to come. It's late and all 10 have fallen asleep. Suddenly they hear someone shouting that the bridegroom is finally coming. They've all been given lamps and oil to help light the way but five of them have run out of oil, and the other five can't lend them any. Those without oil hurry to buy more, but while they're on their way the bridegroom arrives and the wedding banquet begins. Arriving late, they ask the bridegroom to let them in but he claims not to know them and they're denied entrance.

This is another example of how some tribulation survivors will be received into the Kingdom while others will be excluded. The key ingredient here is oil, which symbolizes the Holy Spirit and identifies the five who have it as faithful believers, while those without it are not believers.

Those who try to find the Church in this parable overlook the fact that the timing is all wrong, and the church is the bride, not a bridesmaid. A bride doesn't need the groom's permission to enter her own wedding banquet. Also, characterizing the five without oil as backslidden Church Age believers runs counter to the one condition of our salvation, which is belief, not behavior. And finally, a Church Age believer cannot lose the Holy Spirit, who is sealed within us as a deposit guaranteeing our inheritance. Once again, the Lord warned them to keep watch because they won't know the day or hour of his return (**Matt 25:13**).

The Talents. (Matt. 25:14-30)

Using the word "again" to begin this parable indicates the Lord is still speaking of the time just after His 2nd Coming and that means the servants are Tribulation survivors. It's the story of three servants who were given allotments of money, 5 talents, 2 talents, and 1 talent respectively, by a master who was going away for a time. When He returned he called them in for an accounting. The servants who were given 5 and 2 talents had both doubled their master's money and were commended. The servant given one talent had buried it in the ground and returned it to him untouched. This servant was rebuked. The talent was taken from him and he was thrown into the outer darkness.

Remember, in a parable everything is symbolic. The key to understanding this one lies in discovering what a talent of money symbolizes. Five talents was a lot of money, so the talents must represent something very valuable to the Lord, but there's no indication in the Bible that money is of value to Him. Seeing them as abilities we have is also a mistake because we don't have anything He needs. Even the most "talented" among us can not contribute anything to the Lord's accomplishments. Out of love He sometimes lets us help, but He doesn't need our help. **Job 35:6-8** tells us our sins don't hurt Him and our righteousness doesn't help Him. They only affect us. However, according to **Psalm 138:2** He values His name and His word above all things.

God must fulfill the promises He has made. We call these promises prophecy. He's given His word that He will do all that He says (**Isaiah 46:11**) because His name is at stake (**Ezekiel 36:22-23**). Study His word and your faith will multiply. But ignore it and you'll lose even the little bit with which you began. In the Church Age we're protected against total loss (**1 Cor. 3:15**), but it won't be so afterward. If they don't use His word to multiply their faith, they'll lose it. And they'll lose their place in the Kingdom as well.

The Sheep And The Goats.
(Matt. 25:31-46)

The Lord's final example leaves no doubt as to its timing. *"When the Son of Man comes in his glory, and all the angels with Him, He will sit on his throne in heavenly glory"* (**Matt. 25:31**) It's the time just after the 2nd coming when He will bring all the world's tribulation survivors to stand before Him in judgment. He'll separate them based on how they treated His brothers during the Great Tribulation. Believers, called sheep, will be placed on His right and welcomed into the Millennial Kingdom where they'll help repopulate the Earth. Unbelievers, called goats, will be placed on His left and then thrown into the eternal fire prepared for the devil and his angels.

This appears to be a judgment based on works, but as with everything else the Lord looks at the motive behind our actions. Only a true believer would be willing to take the risks necessary to help protect the Jewish people against the anti-Christ's determined effort to wipe them out to the last one. If he can do this before they petition the Lord's return he will have won, so his extermination efforts will be even more relentless than Hitler's. Anyone caught trying to thwart his effort will share the fate of the Jews. Those who help the Jews will be doing so at their own peril. But it will be as if they are helping the Lord Himself out of gratitude for all He's done for them. Their faith will be rewarded.

After Jesus had told them all these things they joined the

rest of the disciples and continued on their short walk to Bethany, where they were staying.

Wednesday 13 Nisan. The Betrayal

Now the Feast of Unleavened Bread, called the Passover, was approaching, and the chief priests and the teachers of the law were looking for some way to get rid of Jesus, for they were afraid of the people. Then Satan entered Judas, called Iscariot, one of the Twelve. And Judas went to the chief priests and the officers of the temple guard and discussed with them how he might betray Jesus. They were delighted and agreed to give him money. He consented, and watched for an opportunity to hand Jesus over to them when no crowd was present. (**Luke 22:1-6**)

Much has been written about the motives that drove Judas to betray the Lord. Some say His intentions were honorable while others say they weren't, but the Bible is silent on the issue. What it does say is that the betrayal came as no surprise. Jesus had already predicted it.

Then Jesus replied, "Have I not chosen you, the Twelve? Yet one of you is a devil!" (He meant Judas, the son of Simon Iscariot, who, though one of the Twelve, was later to betray him.) (**John 6:70-71**).

Some of the disciples asked Jesus where He wanted to celebrate the Passover because as soon as the sun set it would be Thursday, the 14th of Nisan.

He told them, *"Go into the city, and a man carrying a jar of water will meet you. Follow him. Say to the owner of the house he enters, 'The Teacher asks: Where is my guest room, where*

I may eat the Passover with my disciples?' He will show you a large upper room, furnished and ready. Make preparations for us there." (**Mark 14:13-15**)

Thursday 14 Nisan. The Crucifixion

When evening came, Jesus arrived with the Twelve. While they were reclining at the table eating, he said, "I tell you the truth, one of you will betray me—one who is eating with me."

They were saddened, and one by one they said to him, "Surely not I?"

"It is one of the Twelve," he replied, "one who dips bread into the bowl with me (**Mark 14:17-20**).

John 12:26-30 confirms that it was Judas, who went out to alert the authorities as soon as he had taken the bread. His betrayal was a fulfillment of **Psalm 41:9,** written by David 1,000 years earlier. *Even my close friend, whom I trusted, he who shared my bread, has lifted up his heel against me.*

During the meal, which was eaten in the evening (Jewish days begin at sunset) at the same time Moses and the Israelites had eaten the first Passover in Egypt, Jesus introduced the New Covenant. He took bread and said it represented His body, given for us, and the wine in the cup He held represented His blood, shed for the remission of sin. He said whenever we eat of the bread and drink of the cup we proclaim the Lord's death until He comes (**1 Cor. 11:23-26**). From that day to this, Christians have celebrated communion on a regular basis, each time looking back to the cross, where He died in our place, and forward to the crown, with its promise of eternal life. Paul called it the crown of righteousness, which the Lord will award to all who have longed for His appearing (**2 Tim. 4:8**).

After the meal they went outside the city heading east toward the Mt. Of Olives, where the Garden of Gethsemane was located. It was an olive orchard just across the narrow Kidron Valley from the East Gate of the Temple. On the way, Jesus reminded them of His coming death and told them they'd soon be scattered for fear of the authorities, in fulfillment of **Zechariah 13:7.** But He promised He'd see them again after His resurrection. Peter denied that he'd fall away, even if all the others did. In reply Jesus said *"I tell you the truth, this very night, before the rooster crows, you will disown me three times"* (**Matt. 26:34**) It happened just as He foretold.

When they arrived at the Garden, Jesus told them to wait while He went a little further to pray alone. 1,000 years earlier, David had described what it feels like to be crucified (**Psalm 22:1-18**) and Jesus knew full well the terrible suffering and pain that awaited Him. Three times He asked the Father to not to make Him go through with it if there was any other way to save mankind from their sins. Some theologians call this the unanswered prayer, but the Father's silence was the answer. There was no other way.

Without the shedding of blood there can be no remission

of sin (**Hebr. 9:22**) but the blood of sacrificial animals was not sufficient to the task. It only served to remind the people of their sins (**Hebr. 10:3-4**). It took the blood of a sinless man to redeem sinful mankind once and for all (**Hebr. 10:11-14**). Jesus knew His prayer had been heard when an angel from Heaven came to strengthen Him, and He rose to face His accusers.

A couple of the most obvious indicators of the Lord's control over events happened during the course of His arrest. When the Temple guards arrived, Jesus asked who they were looking for and they replied, "Jesus of Nazareth." Jesus said, "I am He", which caused them all to fall to the ground (**John 18:4-6**). The word "He" doesn't appear in the original text. It was added by the English translators. Jesus only said "I am", the name by which God identified Himself to Moses from the burning bush (**Exodus 3:13-14**).

It was a clear demonstration of His power to singlehandedly defeat them had He chosen to. And as if that wasn't enough, He told Peter He had more than 12 legions of angels at His disposal (**Matt. 26-53**). Since a legion numbered 6,000 troops, that's 72,000 angelic warriors standing by, ready and waiting.

At that point Peter drew a sword and cut off the ear of the High Priest's servant Malchus (**John 18:10**). Jesus touched the man's ear and healed him (**Luke 22:51**), telling Peter to put away his sword, saying all who drew the sword would die by the sword (**Matt. 26:52**).

The word servant is misleading. Malchus was most likely one of the High Priest's most trusted assistants, sent with the guards as his representative to make sure the arrest went as planned. There's no indication he was a believer, nor did he ask to be healed. With this miracle the Lord protected Peter from arrest by reversing the effect of his impulsive act.

By the way, Jesus was not arguing against the taking up of arms in the general sense. It was a reminder that Peter was hopelessly outnumbered by professional soldiers. If he insisted on brandishing his sword, he would surely die from the thrusts of their swords.

That night Jesus endured numerous trials, all of them illegal. The Jews prided themselves in their mercy and only rarely invoked the death penalty. Formal charges always had to be filed before bringing an accused man to trial. Trials were never held in secret or at night. Conviction required a unanimous decision by a court of 70 leaders, and they had a "sleep on it " rule that meant they had to vote again the next day to confirm their decision. Also, it took the confirming testimony of two independent witnesses to establish a man's guilt.

None of this was the case in the Lord's conviction. No formal charges were filed. The group of leaders who tried Him purposely excluded anyone who would have been sympathetic toward Him. He was convicted on His testimony alone, and confined to a cell for an early morning execution. The sleep on it rule was ignored.

When he learned that Jesus had been convicted, Judas, recognizing the terrible mistake he had made, tried to undo it by returning the 30 pieces of silver he'd been paid to betray Jesus. Failing in this he threw the money into the Temple and fled. Because it was tainted, the priests were unable to return the money to the treasury, so they purchased a field to be used as a burial ground from a man who earned his living as a potter (**Matt. 27:6-7**). All this had been foretold in remarkable detail 450 years earlier (**Zechariah 11:12-13**). In his despair Judas took his own life.

Because the Jewish leaders lacked the authority to execute a criminal, Jesus had to be found guilty of a capital crime under Roman law. So they took Him to Pontius Pilate and stated their case. But Pilate was not persuaded. He tried to have Jesus released, but the unruly crowd that had gathered around demanded that Jesus be crucified. The Jewish leaders had stirred them up against Jesus and they weren't going to settle for anything less than His execution. When Pilate insisted that Jesus had done nothing deserving of death, they shouted all the louder, "Crucify Him!" Finally he called for water, and symbolically washing his hands, he said, *"I am innocent of this man's blood. It is your responsibility"* (**Matt. 27:24**).

All the people answered, "Let His blood be on us and on our children!" (**Matt. 27:25**) And so it has been for the last 1980 years. Pilate had Jesus flogged and turned Him over for crucifixion.

The Roman method of flogging was so brutal that many prisoners didn't survive it. When they were finished with Jesus He was in deep shock. Their whips had torn the skin and muscle from His back exposing the bones of His rib cage. But the worst was yet to come.

It was nine AM when Jesus was nailed to the cross and for the next 6 hours He endured the most excruciatingly painful method of execution ever devised. Crucifixion is essentially a death by suffocation. Because the condemned man was hanging by his arms, he couldn't draw a full breath unless he supported His weight with His feet. But pushing against the nails that were driven through his feet was so painful he could only do it for a few seconds at a time, so his lungs slowly filled up with carbon dioxide until he could no longer breathe. **Isaiah 53:4-5** tells us the magnitude of our sins made this brutality necessary to ensure our spiritual and physical healing.

At noon darkness came over the whole land. God had turned away, unable to watch, taking His light from the world as He did. 750 years earlier the prophet Amos had warned them this would happen.

"In that day," declares the Sovereign Lord, "I will make the Sun go down at noon and darken the Earth in broad daylight" (**Amos 8:9**).

Throughout this unspeakable ordeal Jesus had uttered not a whimper. With all the power of the Universe at His command He allowed himself to be led like a lamb to the slaughter (**Isaiah 53:7**). But the pain of being separated from His Father was too much for Him to bear. Finally, at 3 PM He cried out for the first time. *"My God, My God, why have You forsaken Me?"*(**Matt. 27:46**)

Knowing that all was now completed, and so that the Scripture would be fulfilled, Jesus said, "I am thirsty." A jar of wine vinegar was there, so they soaked a sponge in it, put the sponge on a stalk of the hyssop plant, and lifted it to Jesus' lips. When he had received the drink, Jesus said, "It is finished." With that, he bowed his head and gave up his spirit. (**John 19:28–30**)

At the last supper Jesus said He wouldn't drink wine again until the Kingdom came (**Matt. 26:29**), and He had refused a drink of it earlier in the day (**Matt. 27:34**). But now He was asking for one.

Also, the Greek word translated "it is finished" was a commonly used term that meant "paid in full" in normal legal and commercial affairs. The debt of sin mankind owed to God had been paid. Taken together these two things indicate that with the Lord's death phase one of the Kingdom, later to be known as the Church, had come. Accepting a drink of wine confirmed this.

Although it would be several hours before the Lord's body was removed from the cross and placed in a tomb, by 3 PM His Spirit had departed and was in paradise. All four Gospel accounts agree that the Lord's death took place on Preparation Day, as Passover had come to be known (**Matt. 27:62, Mark 15:42, Luke 23:54, John 19:31**).

Christ, our Passover lamb, had been sacrificed (**1 Cor. 5:7**) on Passover.

The Jewish leaders asked Pilate for the crucified men to be off their crosses by sunset when it became the 15th of Nisan, beginning the Feast of Unleavened Bread. It was a special Sabbath on which no work could be done (**Lev. 23:6-7**) and they wanted the crosses to be empty by then (**John 19:31**). Joseph of Arimathea, a wealthy man and a believer in Jesus, asked for and received the Lord's body. He and Nicodemus, another prominent believer, laid it in Joseph's own tomb but were unable to complete the burial process before the sunset brought the Holy Day.

Friday, 15 Nisan. The Feast Of Unleavened Bread.

For most of Israel in Biblical times the 15th of Nisan was a day of celebration and rest, commemorating their release from slavery in Egypt. At the beginning of the 14th they ate a quick ceremonial meal of lamb, unleavened bread and bitter herbs like their ancestors had done. The rabbis said if they consumed a piece of lamb the size of an olive they had met the requirements for the day. Then they spent the rest of the 14th hurriedly preparing for the coming feast. That's why the 14th became known as Preparation Day.

But on the 15th it was a different story, because that's when they ate a large, leisurely meal while they recounted the story of the Exodus. It was an official national holiday on which no regular work could be done.

For the disciples it was a time of mourning. Their teacher, our Redeemer, had been executed and it felt like 3 years of preparation for the coming Kingdom had been for nought. They were also afraid they might hear the sound of soldiers coming for them too, in an effort to completely wipe out all the Lord's followers and put an end to His ministry. Jesus had told them they would weep and mourn while the world around them rejoiced. He said they would grieve, but their grief would turn to joy that no one could take away (**John 16:20-22**). But for now there was only grief.

Unseen to the living, another group was having an even greater celebration than the Jews in Israel. The spirits of Old Testament believers who had died in the hope that a Redeemer would come to pay for their sins had finally met Him. Jesus had promised one of the men being crucified with Him that they'd be together in paradise that very day (**Luke 23:42-43**), and there He was, preaching the Good News that their faith had been justified. He would soon be taking them to Heaven (**Ephes. 4:8**).

For this is the reason the gospel was preached even to those who are now dead, so that they might be judged according to men in regard to the body, but live according to God in regard to the spirit. (**1 Peter 4:6**)

He wasn't there to be tormented by the devil, as some teach, but to announce His victory, a victory in which those in Paradise would soon share. Remember, just before He died, He had said, "It is finished." The price had been paid in full, the work was done. There would be no more suffering.

While He was there He also proclaimed His victory to the spirits in prison who had rebelled against God in the days before the Great Flood (**2 Peter 3:18-20**). Some say these are the fallen angels who are being held in chains while awaiting their final judgment (**Jude 1:6**).

Saturday, 16 Nisan. The Weekly Sabbath

Coming on the heels of the previous day's special sabbath meant that the women were once again prevented from preparing the Lord's body for burial. Had there been a regular work day between the crucifixion and the resurrection they would have prepared the body immediately, as was the custom, and would not have been there on Sunday morning to discover that it was missing.

Sunday, 17 Nisan. The Resurrection, The Feast Of First Fruits

The Feast of First Fruits always came on the day after the Sabbath that followed Passover. As the priests were taking a sample of the harvest to the Temple for dedication, the women were preparing to finish the job Joseph and Nicodemus had begun three days earlier. But when they arrived at the tomb they discovered the Lord's body wasn't there. An angel told them He had risen, just as He said He would, the first fruits of the first resurrection.

Jesus appeared and spoke briefly with Mary Magdalene

outside the tomb that morning, asking her not to hold onto Him because He was going to the Father. The writer of Hebrews tells us He was taking His blood to sprinkle on the altar in Heaven in His capacity as our High Priest (**Hebr. 9:11-12**). This would open the gates of Heaven to all believers. Mary ran back to tell the others, but by the time Peter and John got there the Lord was gone. They both inspected the tomb carefully, amazed to find it was empty.

That afternoon Jesus came alongside 2 of his followers on the road to Emmaus, but they were initially kept from recognizing Him. When He asked why they appeared so downcast, they explained all that had happened concerning Jesus of Nazareth and were surprised that He hadn't heard about it. And what's more, they said, it was the third day since all this had taken place (**Luke 24:13-21**).

That comment alone should have forever put to rest the controversy surrounding the actual day of the Lord's crucifixion. Think about it. It was Sunday, the third day since it happened. That means Saturday would have been the second day since it happened, and Friday was the first day since. That makes Thursday the day it happened.

That evening Jesus appeared to ten of the disciples. (Judas had killed himself and Thomas was absent.) For the first time they received the Holy Spirit (**John 20:19-22**).

Then he opened their minds so they could understand the Scriptures. He told them, "This is what is written: The Christ will suffer and rise from the dead on the third day, and repentance and forgiveness of sins will be preached in his name to all nations, beginning at Jerusalem. You are witnesses of these things. I am going to send you what my Father has promised; but stay in the city until you have been clothed with power from on high" (**Luke 24:45–49**).

In these eight days the Lord lived out the essential doctrine of our faith. Paul would later write, *"For what I received I passed on to you as of first importance: that Christ died for our sins according to the Scriptures, that he was buried, that he was raised on the third day according to the Scriptures."* (**1 Cor. 15:3–4**) Believing this is what makes us Christians. The empty tomb is proof that our faith is not in vain.

Chapter 6

The Redeemer In The Church

They were looking intently up into the sky as he was going, when suddenly two men dressed in white stood beside them. "Men of Galilee," they said, "why do you stand here looking into the sky? This same Jesus, who has been taken from you into heaven, will come back in the same way you have seen him go into heaven" (**Acts 1:10-11**).

Forty days after His resurrection Jesus returned to Heaven. Ten days after that the Holy Spirit came to equip the men He had chosen for the task of taking the Good News of His birth, death, and resurrection to all mankind. At first they concerned themselves mostly with the people of Israel. But soon they were spreading out throughout the region, which meant the message of the Redeemer was being preached to Gentiles as well as Jews.

But the Counselor, the Holy Spirit, whom the Father will send in my name, will teach you all things and will remind you of everything I have said to you (**John 14:26**).

As that happened Church leaders began using letters as a means of staying in touch with groups they had started in different cities and to spread the Good News more effectively. These letters focused primarily on what a believer's response to the Good News should be and contained instructions on how to live as a Christian. Also, God continued the documentation process He had begun 2000 years earlier by commissioning men to record the life and teaching of the Redeemer. He had them write four different accounts, each to a specific audience for a specific purpose. These accounts are called the four Gospels.

God had Matthew write to the Jews to demonstrate that Jesus was Israel's promised Messiah. Mark wrote to the Romans depicting Jesus as the obedient servant of God, sent to Earth for the specific purpose of redeeming mankind. Luke wrote to the Greeks emphasizing the human nature of Jesus as the son of man. And John wrote to the Church to demonstrate the Lord's deity as the Son of God. This is why one Gospel story might contain things others don't, or take a different slant on a particular event than the others. The get the full story you have to read all four.

These four gospels were combined with the letters church leaders were circulating among the churches to form the New Testament. There are 27 documents in the New

Testament and all were written between about 45 and 95 AD by people who were eyewitnesses to the events they were describing. And as He promised, the Lord had the Holy Spirit guide this effort, helping the writers remember everything Jesus told them and making sure they got it right (**John 14:25–26**). For 2,000 years The New Testament has been the primary source of information for the Church to help us understand who the Redeemer is, why we need Him, and how we should live in response to what He's done for us.

Like the Old Testament before it, incredible effort has been expended to make sure the New Testament we read today is a faithful representation of these original writings. Because of that effort New Testament documents are better preserved and more numerous than those of any other ancient writings. There are nearly 6,000 Greek manuscripts in existence today for the New Testament, thousands more than for any other ancient text. Because the copies are so numerous, they can be cross checked for accuracy. This process has determined that the internal consistency of New Testament documents is about 99.5% textually pure. In addition there are over 19,000 copies in the Syriac, Latin, Coptic, and Aramaic languages. The total supporting New Testament manuscript base is over 24,000 manuscripts.

Within a few hundred years the Roman Empire adopted Christianity as its official religion and today there are 2.2 billion people who call themselves Christians, more than there are in any other religion.

As you might expect with sinful mankind, many of these Christians have adopted rules and practices that don't appear in the Bible. Like the Jewish people before them, they can't resist adding to what the Scriptures say and trying to make it appear that if we don't obey their rules then we're not real believers.

None of this surprised God, so He had the New Testament writers make His expectations very clear. For example, one day as Jesus was teaching the people someone asked, *"What must we do to do the work God requires?"*

His answer was unmistakably clear. *"The Work of God is this: to believe in the one He has sent"* (**John 6:28-29**)

Throughout His ministry Jesus emphasized belief as the one condition for salvation. Later Paul summarized the Gospel this way.

"For what I received I passed on to you as of first importance: that Christ died for our sins according to the Scriptures, that he was buried, that he was raised on the third day according to the Scriptures" (**1 Cor. 15:3-4**)

Because we were hopelessly lost and unable to save ourselves from the penalty of our sins, Jesus died in our place and was buried in a tomb. Three days later He was raised to life again, proof that His death had paid the full price for all of our sins.

As soon as we believe that, we are saved from death to eternal life and God sends His Holy Spirit as a deposit to guarantee our inheritance in His Kingdom. He accepts responsibility for us, puts His mark of ownership on us, and seals His spirit in our heart to make sure no power in heaven or on earth can ever undo what Jesus did for us (**2 Cor. 1:21-22**).

If you sincerely believe this Gospel you are saved and your future in eternity is guaranteed. All you have to do is say a simple prayer to confirm your belief and take your place in the forever family of God. You don't have to do anything special to prepare and you don't need any witnesses when you say it. You can even read it silently if you're not in a private place. God hears all our prayers and has been waiting all your life for you to pray this one.

Dear Lord, I know I'm a sinner, unable to save myself. Please forgive my sins and be my Redeemer. I don't ask this because I think I deserve it. I know I don't deserve it. I ask this because you promised that if I believe you came to die for my sins I would not perish but would have eternal life. Thank you for fulfilling your promise to me and letting me spend eternity with you. Amen

If you just prayed that prayer for the first time, congratlations! You're now one of God's children (**John 1:12-13**) and your iheritance is guaranteed in Heaven. And even though you can't hear it, there is rejoicing right now in the presence of the angels of God because of it (**Luke 15:10**).

PART 3.
BUT WAIT THERE'S MORE!

Chapter 7

The Redeemer In Prophecy

"Do not let your hearts be troubled. Trust in God; trust also in me. In my Father's house are many rooms; if it were not so, I would have told you. I am going there to prepare a place for you. And if I go and prepare a place for you, I will come back and take you to be with me that you also may be where I am" (**John 14:1-3**)

I'm sure you'll agree that it would have been enough if Jesus had only redeemed us by going to the cross to pay for our sins. But His death accomplished much more than that. It also made our eternal life in the presence of God possible, because just for believing in Jesus God has given us the authority to become one of His children (**John 1:12-13**). He adopted us into His family, and legally made us one of His heirs (**Galatians 4:4-7**).

To that end, Jesus has spent the last 2, 000 years preparing a place for us in His Father's house. Someone once observed that if God created the world in just 6 days, imagine what He can build in 2,000 years. The Bible only offers a sparse description of this place He's preparing and we'll review that a little later. But for now, notice that He didn't promise to come back here to be with us where we are. He promised to come back to take us there so we can be with Him where He is.

Traditionally, Christians have been taught that when we die we go to Heaven to be with Jesus. But that's only part of the story. To understand all of it we have to realize that as humans we are made up of three components, one we can see and two we can't see. The one we can see is called our body. It's physical and temporary, in that it slowly wears out with age and will eventually cease to function. When that happens we are said to have died.

But it's really only our body that has died. The other two parts of us, called our soul and our spirit, are invisible to us and they will never die. Our soul is the conscious part of us, composed of mind (intellect), will, and emotions. It makes choices and controls our behavior by giving orders to the body. Our spirit is the subconscious part, an internal adviser to the conscious soul. It's sometimes called our conscience. When we become a believer our spirit and the Spirit of God become connected, meaning the advice our spirit gives to our soul now comes directly from God.

When the body of a believer dies, his or her soul and

spirit go to heaven to await the day when they'll receive a new body (**2 Cor. 5:6-8**). This new body will be like the old one, except that it will never wear out and will never cease to function. The reunion of our soul and spirit with our new body is called being raised from the dead. It's our resurrection.

This resurrection will take place at the time Jesus comes back to take us to our new home in His father's house (**1 Thes. 4:16-17**). No one knows exactly when that will happen, but many scholars believe it will take place during our lifetime.

And that leads me to the one exception to the above. In all of human history there will be one generation of believers who will not experience physical death but will pass directly from this life to the next one (**1 Cor. 15:51-53**). The bodies of this generation will be instantaneously changed from mortal (subject to death) to immortal (not subject to death) . This miracle will take place at the same time as the resurrection of believers and is called the rapture, or catching away, of the Church. As I said many scholars believe we are the generation of believers who will experience this.

In one moment we'll be going about our normal lives and in the next we will have disappeared from Earth and will be standing in our eternal home in the presence of the Lord. Along with us will be all the believers who have died since the church began 2,000 years ago. All our believing friends and family who have died will be alive again. We'll recognize them and they'll recognize us. It will be the greatest family reunion in the history of mankind.

But it's even more than that. One of the first things to happen after the rapture will be something called the bema seat judgment. The term bema seat comes from the ancient Olympic games where the bema seat was the equivalent of the modern judges stand on which medals are awarded to the winners of each event. At our bema seat judgment the Lord will award "crowns", to those who qualify, for the effort they've put forth in advancing the work of the Kingdom during their time on Earth as believers (**1 Cor. 3:10-15**).

Then we'll take our place beside Him on His throne where we'll reign with Him and serve as the example for all the ages to come of the incomparable riches of God's grace (**Ephesians 2:6-9**). No other group of humans ever has or ever will enjoy the special relationship we have with our Redeemer. It's unique to the Church.

The only things we must do to qualify for all this is to sincerely believe that Jesus died for our sins and rose again, and ask Him to be our Redeemer.

By the way, don't confuse the building you go to on Sunday or the group of people who join you there with the Church. In the first place, the Church is not a building. But more importantly, the Church is the world wide body of people from all denominations and no denomination who have lived during the last 2,000 years and believe that Jesus died for our sins, was buried, and rose again on the third day, and who have asked Him to be their Savior, their Redeemer. These are the people who will receive the unparalleled blessings the Lord has promised to those who believe.

Chapter 8

The Redeemer Returns

"At that time the sign of the Son of Man will appear in the sky, and all the nations of the earth will mourn. They will see the Son of Man coming on the clouds of the sky, with power and great glory" (**Matt. 24:30**). *The LORD will be king over the whole earth. On that day there will be one LORD, and his name the only name* (**Zechariah 14:9**).

At the beginning of this book we learned of the Lord's promise that His Redeemer will overcome Satan. After He takes the Church to our eternal home, the Lord will enter into a period of judgment against all those who have refused His offer of pardon for their sins, and by doing so have sided with Satan against Him. This judgment will be seven years in duration and has been called the time of God's wrath. Jesus said it will include the worst time of trouble the world ever has or ever will experience, which

He called the Great Tribulation (**Matt. 24:21**). The Bible promises us that the Lord will rescue His church from both the time and place of God's wrath because He doesn't intend for us to suffer through it (**1 Thes. 1:10, 1 Thes. 5:9**). This is the rapture I spoke about earlier.

The judgments will begin as an escalation of things the world is currently experiencing; wars, natural disasters, epidemics, and hunger. In fact the current increase in both the frequency and intensity of these things is an indicator that the time of God's wrath is coming soon. But after the church disappears they will suddenly become much more catastrophic in nature.

As Satan and his forces fight back, there will be a further escalation into supernatural warfare, with mankind caught in the middle of of a great war in the spiritual realm for control of planet Earth. Before it's over half the world's remaining population will have perished and there will hardly be any place on Earth left unblemished by the ferocity of this war. Whole cities will have been leveled, and even mountain ranges will have been flattened, Over much of Earth's surface uncontrolled fires will have burned everything in sight. The smoke from these fires will have literally turned daylight into darkness. Food and fresh water will be in the shortest supply ever.

Things will get so bad that if the Lord didn't put an end to it not a single human would survive. But for the sake of those who will have cried out to Him for mercy, He will put an end to it, and in one final battle He'll defeat the armies arrayed against Him, take Satan prisoner, and restore peace to the world. On that day He will be hailed as the King of the whole earth and even His enemies will bow before Him and acknowledge Him as Lord (**Zechariah 14:9, Philippians 2:9-11**).

He will immediately begin supernaturally restoring the Earth to the condition in which it was originally created (**Acts 3:21**). The world will once again be the paradise God always intended for it to be. In a series of judgments He'll have every unbeliever left alive escorted off the planet to a place of eternal punishment. Living believers will be welcomed into His Kingdom to begin repopulating the Earth, and a time of peace and prosperity like the world has never experienced will begin. There will even be peace between mankind and the animals.

The Lord Himself will rule the Earth, quickly settling all disputes and meting out His perfect justice. The nations of Earth will no longer go to war against each other. In fact they won't even need armies and navies to protect them.

God's creation will flourish during this time of peace. Earthquakes and storms will be a thing of the past. Harvests will be so plentiful that before the farmers can finish gathering up the produce of one season it will be time to plant the seed for the next one. Men will no longer work solely for the benefit of others, but will once again enjoy the fruit of their labors (**Isaiah 65:21-22**).

In the sky above them the New Jerusalem, home of the redeemed Church, will take its station in orbit around the

Earth. The Sun and Moon will have both ceased shining at the end of the Great Tribulation (**Matt. 24:29**) and with the Lord's victorious return the New Jerusalem will have descended out of Heaven to become the Earth's source of light (**Rev. 21:23-24**).

The Church's eternal home will be a magnificent structure unequaled in man's history. No one knows its exact shape, but it will be about 1400 miles high, 1400 miles wide, and 1400 miles deep (**Rev. 21:16**), or about 2/3rds the size of the moon. Some have estimated that we'll each have about 10,000 square feet of the most luxurious living space ever made there. It will be constructed entirely of gold, so pure as to be nearly transparent, and the entire structure will be adorned by untold numbers of precious gems. Even its streets will be made of the finest gold (**Rev. 21:18-21**). Nothing impure will ever enter it, only those whose names are written in the Redeemer's Book of Life documenting their membership in His Church (**Rev. 21:27**).

God always intended that in our immortal bodies we would be conformed to the likeness of His son (**Romans 8:29**). We don't know exactly what that means, but the Bible tells us when He appears to us we'll be like Him, able to see Him as He is (**1 John 3:2**).

He'll wipe every tear from our eyes. There will be no more death or mourning or crying or pain for the old order of things will have passed away (**Rev. 21:4**). A new day, eternal in its duration, will have dawned.

All this has been determined for us, guaranteed to all who believe that when the Redeemer came to die for the sins of the people, His death paid for all our sins. In other words, being the Savior of the world, He is also our personal Savior. When we accept Him as such, He credits all these blessings to our benefit and makes it so no power in Heaven or on Earth can ever take them away from us.

The Bible only describes the first 1,000 years of God's Kingdom. But in several places it says that His Kingdom will be an eternal one, a kingdom that will never be destroyed or left to another people, but will endure forever (**Daniel 2:44**).

With one simple heart-felt decision you can be part of it. If you haven't already done so, make that decision today. The Redeemer came to Earth to die for your sins so you could have eternal life in Heaven with Him. It's a free gift from Him to everyone who believes. All you have to do is ask for it to receive it (**Matt. 7:7-8**). Of all the things you can do that promise to change your life, this one really will. In fact it will change your eternal destiny.

PART 4.
IT'S WHAT YOU LEARN AFTER
YOU THINK YOU KNOW IT ALL
THAT REALLY MATTERS

Important Topical Studies For Growth and Understanding

Therefore, dear friends, since you already know this, be on your guard so that you may not be carried away by the error of lawless men and fall from your secure position. But grow in the grace and knowledge of our Lord and Savior Jesus Christ. To him be glory both now and forever! Amen (**2 Peter 3:17-18**).

What follows are some topical studies to help provide answers for questions you might have, based on your reading so far. They are not meant to be all inclusive, but will get you off to a good start in your quest to become more familiar with God's word. They are a sample of over 1,000 similar studies on our webite www.gracethrufaith. com. (The site also includes answers to over 7,000 questions on every Bible topic you can think of.)

Taking time to study the Bible is the most important thing a believer can do, because it can help give us a view of our life based on the promises God has made to us, rather than blindly going along with the view that's been handed down to us by the world.

Most people don't understand that we all live forever. Our bodies will wear out and cease to function, but the parts of us that are really us, our soul and our spirit, will keep on living. So the real question is not whether we have eternal life, but how and where we're going to spend eternity. Those who choose to accept the pardon Jesus purchased for us with His life will spend it with Him in a state of continuous blessing. Those who don't accept His pardon will live a life of separation from God in a state of eternal punishment.

God loves us and doesn't want anyone to suffer this punishment. He would prefer that everyone would accept the pardon He made available (**2 Peter 3:9**) and that's why He made it free for the asking (**Matt. 7:7-8**). But He is also just and because of that He can't overlook our sins. If we don't let Jesus pay for them on our behalf, then we have to pay for them ourselves. It's that simple.

Because most people don't understand these things, they spend all their time and energy trying to make this life as good as they can. They think it's the only life they have. That's because they don't read the Bible, which is the only guide we've been given to help us develop an eternal perspective. But this life will only last 70-80 years for the average person. That's such a small percentage of eternity as to be insignificant.

Please don't get the idea that we can either have a good life here or a good life in eternity, because the Bible promises both. By reading the Bible and learning about God's promises to us we can have an abundant life here (**John 10:10**) and an eternal life with the Lord that's so great our minds can't begin to imagine it. The Apostle Paul once wrote, *"No eye has seen, no ear has heard, no mind has conceived what God has prepared for those who love Him"* (**1 Cor. 2:9**) because it's beyond our comprehension.

By reading these studies and checking the references I've included to help you be sure I've got my facts straight, you can get enough of a glimpse into both the earthly phase and the eternal phase of a believer's life to know beyond a doubt that it's the life for you.

That said, let's get you started with some basic studies that will help you understand your life in Christ more clearly. They're in no particular order and each one can be studied independently of the others. So pick any one you want and take all the time you need.

1. Messianic Prophecy In The Old Testament

A Bible Study by Jack Kelley

In the time after their sin and expulsion from the Garden Adam and Eve must have felt incredible despair. They had experienced life both before and after the curse, the only ones to do so, and had first hand knowledge of the difference. And what a difference it was. Even the part of it we can relate to had to have been devastating.

For example suppose that one day you were the resident manager of the world's richest and most luxurious estate, with all of its comforts and privileges, and the next you were a poor hardscrabble farmer, at the opposite end of the economic and social structure. And that was just the beginning. How about no longer being immortal, no longer one with your Creator in spirit.

The Seed Of The Woman

To keep them from becoming incurably despondent, God had promised them a Redeemer. In **Genesis 3:15** we read,

And I will put enmity between you and the woman, and between your offspring (seed) and hers; he will crush your head, and you will strike his heel."

He was speaking to the one indwelling the serpent and in Hebrew the promise contains a biological impossibility. Seed comes from the male. It's the Bible's first hint of a virgin birth. An offspring of the woman's would destroy Satan and reverse the consequences of the act he had manipulated, redeeming mankind from its bondage to sin.

Two chapters later in **Genesis 5** the Bible gives us another hint of this. The Hebrew root words of the names of the 10 patriarchs listed there form a sentence. When taken in order it reads like this in English.

"Man is appointed mortal sorrow, but the blessed God will come down teaching that His death will bring the despairing rest."

It's a prophecy that God Himself would come to Earth as the Seed of the Woman, and man's Redeemer.

Centuries later, this was confirmed by the Prophet Isaiah.

For to us a child is born, to us a son is given, and the government will be on his shoulders. And he will be called Wonderful, Counselor, Mighty God, Everlasting Father, Prince of Peace. (**Isaiah 9:6**)

As New Testament believers, we can see that the five names listed here describe all three members of the Trinity. Wonderful is the name by which The Angel of the Lord identified Himself while visiting Samson's parents. (**Judges 13:18**). When the phrase "The Angel of the Lord" appears in the Old testament, it's in conjunction with a pre-incarnate visit by the Lord Jesus. That He's being referenced in **Isaiah 9:6** is confirmed by the title,

Prince of Peace. Jesus called the Holy Spirit the Counselor in **John 14:26** , and Mighty God and everlasting Father can only refer to God.

A Descendant Of Abraham

In **Genesis 12:1-3** the origin of this Redeemer becomes clearer. There God promised Abraham that all the nations of Earth would be blessed through him, and in **Genesis 22** He had Abraham act this out with the sacrifice of Isaac, Abraham's "only son" on Mt. Moriah. 2000 years later another Father would offer His only Son as a sacrifice for sin in that same place. Abraham knew this and named the place Jehovah Jireh, saying, *"On the mountain of the Lord it will be provided"* (**Gen. 22:14**).

The Lion Of Judah

Later, as Abraham's grandson Jacob neared death, he narrowed it down still more by saying that all of Israel's kings including the ultimate one, "the one to whom it (the ruler's staff) belongs", would come from among the descendants of one of his sons, Judah, (**Gen. 49:10**) giving birth to the title "Lion of Judah" as a Messianic reference.

The Son Of David

In **2 Samuel 7:12-15** we read that David longed to build a Temple for God, but God refused him, saying that it would take a man of peace to build a house for Him. He said that David's son Solomon would be that man, and during Solomon's reign Israel experienced peace as never before or since. But to ease David's disappointment God promised to build him a "house" and the Davidic Dynasty was founded. Hence forth there would always be a direct descendant of David's on the throne of Israel. It was an everlasting promise made in about 1000 BC, and Solomon would be the first fulfillment. But since neither Solomon nor any other Davidic King was flogged by men for "doing wrong" (**2 Sam. 7:14**) there's a lot more going on here than meets the eye. The wording casts shadows of the Messiah.

So through God's progressive revelation we've narrowed things down from learning that the Redeemer would be a son of Eve's, which would exclude no one, to the family of Abraham, then Judah, then David. But we're not finished yet. Over the next 400 years the Davidic Kings went from bad to worse with few exceptions. Finally, in the time of the Prophet Jeremiah God had had enough and pronounced a blood curse on the Davidic line, saying that no son of then King Jehoiachin would ever rule over Israel. (**Jere. 22:30**) The Davidic line, begun with Solomon, was seemingly ended and God's promise to David broken.

The Branch

However, before the nation was taken to Babylon, while a Davidic King still sat on the throne, God had Ezekiel announce that the line was being suspended and wouldn't be restored until "He comes to whom it rightfully belongs." (**Ezekiel 21:27**) recalling Jacob's prophecy to mind. In

519 BC, after the Jews had returned from the Babylonian captivity, God said that a man He called The Branch would be the one, and that He would hold the priesthood as well, combining the two. (**Zechariah 6:12**).

There are four references to The Branch in the Old Testament and all point to the Messiah. In **Zechariah 3:8** He's called God's servant, in **Zechariah 6:12** He's a man, both king and priest. In **Jeremiah 23:5** He's called a righteous king, and in **Isaiah 4:2** He's the Branch 0f God.

Born Of a Virgin, Born In Bethlehem

But how was God going to get around the blood curse? For the answer to that, we have to back up to about 750 BC. In that time two of the most specific Messianic prophecies ever given narrowed the field down to just one possibility. In **Isaiah 7:14** the Lord proclaimed that the Messiah would be born of a virgin, and in **Micah 5:2** that he would be born in Bethlehem, the City of David.

In order to legally qualify for a seat on David's throne, the Messiah King would have to be of the house and lineage of David. To be from the house of David means being a biological descendant of David's. Being of David's lineage means belonging to the Royal Line. How can this be?

When we read the Lord's genealogies in **Matt. 1** and **Luke 3**, we can see differences beginning at the time of David. Matthew's genealogy runs through Solomon, the cursed royal line. But Luke's goes through Solomon's brother Nathan. Nathan's line wasn't cursed, but neither were they kings. Further study reveals that Matthew is actually giving us Joseph's genealogy while Luke shows us Mary's. Both were descended from David, and in addition Joseph was one of many who were heir to David's throne but unable to claim it because of the curse on his line.

So through His mother Mary, Jesus was a biological descendant of David's. When Mary and Joseph became husband and wife, Jesus also became Joseph's legal son and heir to David's Throne. But not being biologically related to Joseph, He didn't have the blood curse. He was of both the house and lineage of David. To this day He's the only man born in Israel since 600BC with a legitimate claim to David's throne. The angel Gabriel confirmed this to Mary when he told her that although a virgin, she would soon give birth to the Son of God, who would occupy it forever. (**Luke 1:32-33**) **Isaiah 9:7** had revealed the same fact centuries earlier. God's promise to David stands.

Daniel And The Magi

200 years after Micah identified Bethlehem as the Messiah's birthplace, The Lord told Daniel the time of His death. It would be 483 years after the decree to rebuild and restore Jerusalem following the Babylonian captivity, but before an enemy army came to destroy it again. (**Daniel 9:24-27**) This places the Messiah's death somewhere between 32 and 70 AD according to our reckoning of time.

Daniel formed a group of Persian priests to pass this information down from father to son, and according to tradition set aside the bulk of his personal wealth as a gift for them to present to the Messiah when the time came for His birth. He apparently also gave them a confirming sign to look for from **Numbers 24:17**, later known as the Star of Bethlehem.

The descendants of these priests, now a very influential political force in Parthia (as Persia came to be known), remained true to Daniel's commission, and upon seeing the star set out for Jerusalem. Arriving there they sought an audience with King Herod, asking for the whereabouts of the one born to be King of Israel. Summoning the chief priests, Herod repeated the question and was referred to **Micah 5:2** where Bethlehem is identified. The Parthian priests, or Magi as we call them, went there and found the baby Jesus.

The field of candidates for Redeemer of Mankind, the Seed of the Woman, the Descendant of Abraham, the Lion of Judah, the Son of David, the Messiah of Israel, had been narrowed down to one. His name is Jesus.

Faith In Action

By faith, with nothing more than Daniel's word to their ancestors, the Magi mounted up and undertook a dangerous 800 mile trip into enemy territory to meet the Messiah. (The Parthians and Romans were technically at war.) With 4000 years of fulfilled prophetic scripture in their hands, the chief priests, who no longer took it literally, refused to join them for the last 5 miles from Jerusalem to Bethlehem to see if God's Word really was true. In so doing, the leaders of the people He came to save missed out on the central event in human history, consigning themselves to eternal separation from the very God they had been seeking.

If history repeats itself like they say it does, then when He comes back many of today's religious experts, who also don't take the prophecies literally, will make the same mistake. As you recall the Reason for the Season, take time to thank Him for making you like the Magi instead of like them, because if you listen carefully, you can almost hear the footsteps of the Messiah.

2. The Virgin Mary Had A Baby Boy

A Bible Study by Jack Kelley

Therefore the Lord Himself will give you a sign. The virgin shall be with child and will give birth to a son, and will call him Immanuel (**Isaiah 7:14**).

There is perhaps no prophecy in the Old Testament more controversial than this one. Many liberal theologians reject the notion of the virgin birth of Jesus as being simply legend, Jews flatly deny its validity and non-believers scoff at it as the best example of the mindless belief necessary for Christianity to flourish.

Yet a careful study of the history of Israel, the laws of inheritance, and the promises by God to King David lead even the most skeptical student to conclude that Jesus had to be supernaturally conceived to be both God and human, and therefore qualified to redeem mankind, and have a legitimate claim to the Throne of Israel.

The God Man

Jesus had to be God to forgive our sins. No mere human can do that. One of the charges levied against Him was that He committed blasphemy by claiming the authority to forgive us, a power reserved for God alone (**Mark 2:1-7**). To prove He had that authority, Jesus healed a paralytic (**Mark 2:8-12**) right before His accusers' eyes. The immediate healing was incontrovertible evidence of His authority, derived as a direct descendant of God.

But He had to be human to redeem us. The laws of redemption required that a next of kin redeem that which was lost. (**Lev. 25:24-25**) This so-called kinsman Redeemer had to be qualified, able and willing to perform the act of redemption. When Adam lost dominion over planet Earth and plunged all his progeny into sin, only his next of kin could redeem the Earth and its inhabitants. Since Adam was a human whose Father was God (**Luke 3:23-38**), only another direct Son of God could qualify. This is why Paul referred to Jesus as the last Adam (**1 Cor. 15:45**).

Since the Laws of sacrifice required the shedding of innocent blood as the coin of redemption, only a sinless man was able (**John 1:29-34**). Since the kinsman Redeemer's life was required, only someone who loves us the way God does would be willing (**John 3:16**). This is the real test of the kinsman Redeemer. Seeing Jesus as qualified and able to redeem us isn't a great problem. After all He's the Son of God. But recognizing that He was also willing to step down from His Heavenly Throne to trade His perfect life for ours should really humble us. What kind of love did it take to voluntarily suffer the pain and humiliation required to redeem us?

The Man Who Would Be King

To my logical mind the issue of royalty is the most intriguing factor related to the virgin birth. The opposite of the mindless belief of which Christians are accused, this one is blatantly logical. Does Jesus have a legitimate claim to the Throne of David under the rules of succession? The answer hinges on two technicalities.

First, God promised David that someone from His family would reign in Israel forever. David wanted to build God's house, but God declined, saying He needed a man of peace and David was a man of war. So God chose David's son Solomon to build the Temple and during Solomon's reign Israel experienced peace as never before (or since). To alleviate David's disappointment, God promised to build him a "house" by making his dynasty everlasting (**1 Chron. 17:1-14**). From that time forward a descendant of David's through Solomon's branch of the family tree would sit on the throne in Jerusalem as King of Israel. But by the time of the Babylonian captivity 400 years later, these kings had become so evil and rebellious toward God that He finally said, "Enough", and cursed the royal line, saying no son of their line would ever reign over Israel again (**Jer. 22:28-30**). The last legitimate King of Israel was Jehoiachin, also called Jeconiah, who reigned for only 3 months in 598 BC. Did God break His promise to David?

The second technicality involves the right of inheritance in Israel. God had ordained that Israelites could never sell or give away the allotment of land given to their families during the time of Joshua. *"The land is mine,"* He declared, *"You are but tenants."* (**Lev. 25:23**) It's from this declaration that the rules of inheritance and redemption came forth. Family land was passed from father to son through the generations. If a son lost his land, his brother was to redeem it, so the family wouldn't lose their inheritance. So far so good.

Read The Fine Print

At the end of the Book of Numbers an interesting loophole emerged. A man died without a son, leaving 4 daughters. They came to Moses complaining that they would lose the family land since there was no son to inherit it. Moses sought the Lord, Who decreed that if there was no son in a family daughters could inherit family land providing they married within their own tribal clan. In effect they had to marry a cousin to keep the land "in the family." This made sense since land was allotted first by tribe then by clan then by family. Marrying within the tribal clan kept the families in close proximity and preserved the tribal allotment. (**Numbers 36 1:13**)

Now compare the 2 genealogies of Jesus in **Matthew 1:1-17** and **Luke 3:23-38**, and you'll discover an interesting bit of information. Matthew's account goes forward in time from Abraham and shows that Joseph descended through Solomon, the royal but cursed line, and his father is listed as Jacob. But Luke's account goes backward from Jesus to Adam. In **Luke 3:23** Joseph's father is called Heli, and the line is different all the way to Solomon's brother Nathan before joining Matthew's account at King David. It turns out that Heli was Mary's father and therefore Joseph's father in law. Both Mary and Joseph were descendants of King David.

Here's the tricky part. Mary had no brothers and so was

entitled to inherit her family's land as long as she married someone also descended from David. Remember, this had been spelled out in Numbers 36.

Joseph fit the bill and being in the royal line had a claim to the throne. But like everyone in the royal line, he also carried the blood curse. No biological son of his could ever legally qualify as Israel's king, However, Joseph could secure both Mary's right of inheritance to her family's land and her son's claim to David's throne by marrying her.

When Mary accepted Joseph's offer of marriage she preserved her family's land and also made good her son's claim to the throne of Israel. Her son Jesus legally became Joesph's son as well. This made Jesus an heir to the throne but since he wasn't Joseph's biological son, He escaped the curse. He was a biological descendant of David's through his mother and therefore of the "house and lineage of David."

This whole issue revolves around the facts that; a) God has bound Himself to His own laws, and b) He keeps His word. These are facts that should give you great comfort.

God is not a man that He should lie, nor a son of man that He should change His mind (**Num. 23:19**). Legally, a virgin birth was required to produce a sinless man who would be qualified and able to serve as our Kinsman Redeemer, and God longed to redeem us. A virgin birth was also required to sidestep the blood curse on the royal line, fulfilling God's promise to David that a biological descendant of his would sit on the throne of Israel forever.

We'll Return After This Pause

But what about the 2500 years that have passed since Israel had a King? Remember Jehoiachin was Israel's last real King. In **Ezekiel 21:25-27**, written while a descendant of David's still sat on the throne in Jerusalem, God declared that He was suspending the Davidic line of succession "until He comes to whom it rightfully belongs" a clear reference to the Redeemer. This declaration was confirmed to Mary. The Angel Gabriel promised that her coming son would sit on David's throne and rule over the house of Jacob (Israel) forever (**Luke 1:30-33**).

All during the life of Jesus, a member of the Herod family served as King of Israel. Herod was an Idumean (Jordanian), a friend of Caesar's who was appointed to serve as King. So this promised reinstatement is still to come. It will be fulfilled at the 2nd Coming when "the Son of Man comes in His glory and all the angels with him" to "sit on His throne in heavenly glory". Finally "the Lord will be King over the whole Earth." (**Matt. 25:31** & **Zech. 14:4-9**).

3. The True Identity Of Jesus Of Nazareth.

A Bible Study by Jack Kelley

Of all the so-called holy books, only the Bible authenticates itself. It does so through a method we call predictive prophecy and it works like this. Only God knows the end from the beginning. To help us learn to believe Him, He told His ancient people things that hadn't happened yet. Then when they came to pass just like He said they would, He had them document everything and preserve it for future generations. We call this documentation the Bible, which by many accounts consists of nearly 30% predictive prophecy, some fulfilled and some still to come.

When asked what work God requires of us, Jesus replied, *"The work of God is this. Believe in the One He has sent."* (**John 6:28-29**) Because He's told us so many things in advance and has always been right, He expects us to believe in Him. His view is that He's proven Himself so far beyond any reasonable doubt that people who say they don't believe in Him are really being disobedient by refusing to believe. And belief is a requirement. That's why in the New Testament one of the Greek words translated unbelief also means disobedient.

The Old Testament is so chock full of the proof of God's existence that there's simply no justification for unbelief. (In my study entitled "Proving the Existence Of God" I used the examples of Cyrus the Persian and Alexander the Great to show that anyone with a Study Bible and a competent history book can verify the existence of God simply by comparing fulfilled prophecy with world history.)

The fool says in his heart, "There is no God."(**Psalm 14:1**). Only a fool can say that. But even a fool can't say it logically, with his mind, because there's too much evidence to the contrary. He has to say it emotionally, in his heart. Foolish opinions based on emotion don't need to be true.

What's The Point?

Of all the things we should believe about God, the most important one is that He sent His Son to die for our sins so we could spend eternity with Him. The first prophecy of this appears in **Genesis 3:15** and it's repeated through out the Old Testament.

Can we prove beyond a reasonable doubt that He's done this? After all He's asked us to risk our entire eternity on this issue alone, and by the time we find out for sure if He was telling the truth or not, it will be too late. We'll be dead. It's pretty important that we know for certain.

So let's review a few of the better known prophecies relating to Jesus of Nazareth and see if we can prove that He's the One God sent. And while we're at it, let's see if there's any possibility that he could have fulfilled these prophecies accidentally. Chance is always the rival conjecture. Could this have all happened by coincidence, or can we know that Jesus is the promised Redeemer?

It's About Time

By the way, all the prophecies we'll be looking at are from the Old Testament. I'll give you the approximate date of each one, but if you're worried about the differences of opinion surrounding these dates, make it easy on yourself. It's a fact of history that Ptolemy Philadelphus II had the Hebrew Scriptures translated into Greek beginning in about 282 BC. They didn't do it all at once, but by 150 BC the work was pretty much complete and so each prophecy we'll look at was a matter of public record at least 150 years before the fact. With that, let's get started.

Born Of A Virgin

The Lord had Isaiah tell us that the Messiah would be born of a virgin. This would make Him unique among all men and clearly identify Him as the One God was sending. Isaiah wrote the following passage about 750 BC.

Prophecy: *Therefore the Lord himself will give you a sign: The virgin will be with child and will give birth to a son, and will call him Immanuel.* (**Isaiah 7:14**)

Fulfillment: *The angel said to her, "Do not be afraid, Mary, you have found favor with God. You will be with child and give birth to a son, and you are to give him the name Jesus. He will be great and will be called the Son of the Most High. The Lord God will give him the throne of his father David, and he will reign over the house of Jacob forever; his kingdom will never end."*

"How will this be," Mary asked the angel, "since I am a virgin?" The angel answered, "The Holy Spirit will come upon you, and

the power of the Most High will overshadow you. So the holy one to be born will be called the Son of God. (**Luke 1:30–35**)

Probability of coincidental fulfillment: Impossible to calculate. But since there were about 300 million people alive on Earth when Jesus was born, let's say 1 in 300 million.

Born in Bethlehem

Micah was a contemporary of Isaiah's, also writing about 750 BC. The Lord had him identify the place where the Messiah would be born.

Prophecy: *But you, Bethlehem Ephrathah, though you are small among the clans of Judah, out of you will come for me one who will be ruler over Israel, whose origins are from of old, from ancient times.* (**Micah 5:2**)

Fulfillment: *So Joseph also went up from the town of Nazareth in Galilee to Judea, to Bethlehem the town of David, because he belonged to the house and line of David. He went there to register with Mary, who was pledged to be married to him and was expecting a child. While they were there, the time came for the baby to be born, and she gave birth to her firstborn, a son. She wrapped him in cloths and placed him in a manger, because there was no room for them in the inn.* (**Luke 2:4–7**)

Probability of coincidental fulfillment: Bethlehem has always been a small town. Of Earth's total population, if 3000 people lived in Bethlehem at that time, then the likelihood of a child being born in Bethlehem would have been about 1 in 100,000.

Rides Into Jerusalem On A Donkey

Zechariah wrote after the return from Babylon. His first 8 chapters were written at the beginning of his ministry in 519 and 518 BC and chapters 9-14 at the end of his career, around 480 BC.

Prophecy: *Rejoice greatly, O Daughter of Zion! Shout, Daughter of Jerusalem! See, your king comes to you, righteous and having salvation, gentle and riding on a donkey, on a colt, the foal of a donkey.* (**Zech 9:9**)

Fulfillment: *As he approached Bethphage and Bethany at the hill called the Mount of Olives, he sent two of his disciples, saying to them, "Go to the village ahead of you, and as you enter it, you will find a colt tied there, which no one has ever ridden. Untie it and bring it here. If anyone asks you, 'Why are you untying it?' tell him, 'The Lord needs it.'"*

Those who were sent ahead went and found it just as he had told them. As they were untying the colt, its owners asked them, "Why are you untying the colt?"

They replied, "The Lord needs it."

They brought it to Jesus, threw their cloaks on the colt and put Jesus on it. As he went along, people spread their cloaks on the road.

When he came near the place where the road goes down the Mount of Olives, the whole crowd of disciples began joyfully to praise God in loud voices for all the miracles they had seen: "Blessed is the king who comes in the name of the Lord! Peace in heaven and glory in the highest!" (**Luke 19:29-39**)

Probability of coincidental fulfillment: The population of Jerusalem 2000 years ago was about 50,000 but it being Passover, pilgrims from all over the Middle East would be arriving and would have swelled the number to many times that. It's said that 100,000 lambs were sacrificed that Passover so using the ratio from Exodus of one lamb for every 10 people would mean that upwards of 1 million people crowded into Jerusalem and its surrounding area for the Passover. (Remember every able-bodied Jewish male in the world was required to celebrate Passover in Jerusalem.) Now, what's the likelihood that any one of them, while riding into town on a donkey that first Palm Sunday would cause the crowd to spontaneously hail him as the Messianic King of Israel? We can only guess. 1 in 1 million?

Betrayed For 30 Pieces Of Silver And The Money Used To Buy A Potter's Field

Again, this prophecy of Zechariah's was written about 480 BC.

Prophecy: *I told them, "If you think it best, give me my pay; but if not, keep it." So they paid me thirty pieces of silver. And the LORD said to me, "Throw it to the potter"-the handsome price at which they priced me! So I took the thirty pieces of silver and threw them into the house of the LORD to the potter.* (**Zech 11:12-13**)

Fulfillment: *Then one of the Twelve—the one called Judas Iscariot—went to the chief priests and asked, "What are you willing to give me if I hand him over to you?" So they counted* *out for him thirty silver coins. From then on Judas watched for an opportunity to hand him over.* (**Matt 26:14–16**)

When Judas, who had betrayed him, saw that Jesus was condemned, he was seized with remorse and returned the thirty silver coins to the chief priests and the elders. "I have sinned," he said,"for I have betrayed innocent blood."

"What is that to us?" they replied. "That's your responsibility."

So Judas threw the money into the temple and left. Then he went away and hanged himself.

The chief priests picked up the coins and said, "It is against the law to put this into the treasury, since it is blood money." So they decided to use the money to buy the potter's field as a burial place for foreigners. (**Matt 27:3–7**)

Probability of coincidental fulfillment: This one's also impossible to calculate. It's hard enough to get someone to write about you 500 years before you're born, but then you have to get your betrayer and your sworn enemies to cooperate in fulfilling what's been written. Someone once said that the likelihood of coincidental fulfillment of this prophecy would be like covering the State of Texas with silver dollars to a depth of three feet, randomly marking one of them, and then having a blindfolded person wander around across the state and on his first try, pick up the marked coin. But let's be generous and give it a 1 in 1 million chance.

Though Innocent Made No Defense

This prophecy comes from the Book of Isaiah, written about 750 BC.

Prophecy: *He was oppressed and afflicted, yet he did not open his mouth; he was led like a lamb to the slaughter, and as a sheep before her shearers is silent, so he did not open his mouth.* (**Isaiah 53:7**)

Fulfillment: *Meanwhile Jesus stood before the governor, and the governor asked him, "Are you the king of the Jews?"*

"Yes, it is as you say," Jesus replied.

When he was accused by the chief priests and the elders, he gave no answer. Then Pilate asked him, "Don't you hear the testimony they are bringing against you?" But Jesus made no reply, not even to a single charge—to the great amazement of the governor. (**Matt 27:11-14**)

Probability of coincidental fulfillment: As with the previous example, I don't know of a single person who wouldn't defend himself before his accusers, especially if he was innocent. I know I would protest long and loud at the injustice of false accusation. Above all, it's a violation of the 9th Commandment. If there were 1 million people in Jerusalem that day and if He was the only one who wouldn't defend himself when charged with a capital crime then the probability is 1 in 1 million.

He Was Punished For Our Sins

This is another promise the Lord had Isaiah write down in about 750 BC and one of the most crucial for us to prove.

Prophecy: *But he was pierced for our transgressions, he was crushed for our iniquities; the punishment that brought us peace was upon him, and by his wounds we are healed.* (**Isaiah 53:5**)

Fulfillment: This had been described as a primary goal of the Messiah through out the Old Testament and from the beginning of His ministry, Jesus was identified as the One Who takes away the sins of the people (**John 1:29**) But did he?

After His death the Apostle Paul would write, *God made him who had no sin to be sin for us, so that in him we might become the righteousness of God.* (**2 Cor 5:21**) and *When you were dead in your sins and in the uncircumcision of your sinful nature, God made you alive with Christ. He forgave us all our sins, having canceled the written code, with its regulations, that was against us and that stood opposed to us; he took it away, nailing it to the cross.* (**Colossians 2:13-14**) The Apostle Peter agreed. *For Christ died for sins once for all, the righteous for the unrighteous, to bring you to God.* (**1 Peter 3:18**) Both these men died horrible deaths rather than change even a word of their testimony and are reliable witnesses. As Peter said, "We were eyewitnesses of His majesty."

Probability of coincidental fulfillment: Using our

Jack Kelley

300 million number for the inhabitants of Earth, could you find 300 men who had never sinned and could be convinced that by dying the horrible death of crucifixion, the sins of mankind would be forgiven? If you could the probability is 1 in 1 million.

The Clincher

In **Daniel 9:26** we find the most specific prophecy of all. It was written just as the Babylonian captivity was ending, about 530 BC. In it The Angel Gabriel explained to Daniel that the Messiah would come to Israel and be executed in a narrow window of time between the 483rd year after permission to rebuild Jerusalem was granted and the subsequent destruction of the city and Temple. From history we know that this time frame was 38 years in duration.

Prophecy: *Seventy 'sevens' are decreed for your people and your holy city to finish transgression, to put an end to sin, to atone for wickedness, to bring in everlasting righteousness, to seal up vision and prophecy and to anoint the most holy.*

Know and understand this: From the issuing of the decree to restore and rebuild Jerusalem until the Anointed One, the ruler, comes, there will be seven 'sevens,' and sixty-two 'sevens.' It will be rebuilt with streets and a trench, but in times of trouble. After the sixty-two 'sevens,' the Anointed One will be cut off and will have nothing. The people of the ruler who will come will destroy the city and the sanctuary. (**Daniel 9:24–26**)

Fulfillment: *When he came near the place where the road goes* *down the Mount of Olives, the whole crowd of disciples began joyfully to praise God in loud voices for all the miracles they had seen: "Blessed is the king who comes in the name of the Lord! Peace in heaven and glory in the highest!"*

Some of the Pharisees in the crowd said to Jesus, "Teacher, rebuke your disciples!"

"I tell you," he replied, "if they keep quiet, the stones will cry out."

As he approached Jerusalem and saw the city, he wept over it and said, "If you, even you, had only known on this day what would bring you peace—but now it is hidden from your eyes." (**Luke 19:37–42**)

It was the first Palm Sunday, the only day in His entire ministry when the Lord allowed the people to call Him Israel's King. It was the 10th of Nisan, 483 years to the day after Persian King Artaxerxes Longimonus signed a decree authorizing Nehemiah to go and begin rebuilding Jerusalem. (**Nehemiah 2:1–6**) It was the day ordained in history for the Messiah to arrive in Jerusalem. When they missed it, He prophesied the destruction of the city.

The days will come upon you when your enemies will build an embankment against you and encircle you and hem you in on every side. They will dash you to the ground, you and the children within your walls. They will not leave one stone on another, because you did not recognize the time of God's coming to you. (**Luke 19:43–44**)

38 years later the Romans destroyed the city and tore

the Temple apart stone by stone until not one was left standing on another. Another case of predictive prophecy fulfilled.

What's It All Mean?

If you're looking for the Messiah, you have to find someone who fulfilled not only the seven prophecies we've listed here but all the 300 or so others given in the Old Testament as well. And then He had to give His life for us within the 38 year window of time God revealed to Daniel.

The probability of one man fulfilling just these seven prophecies by chance is 1 in 9 X 10 to the 45th power. That's 1 chance out of 9 with 45 zeros after it. In other words it's so small as to be unworthy of consideration. The true identity of Jesus of Nazareth is that He's Israel's Messiah and our Redeemer. That fact can be proven with greater certainty than you can prove that you are who you claim to be.

OSAS, The Whole Story

A Bible Study by Jack Kelley

If you follow our "Ask a Bible Teacher" feature, you know how many comments I've received lately that question the Doctrine of Eternal Security (aka Once Saved Always Saved or OSAS). Based on their content I've concluded that many people neither understand OSAS nor have they considered the alternative.

Let's Begin At The Beginning

It's time to set the record straight once and for all. What does it take to be saved? I think the best answer to that question is the one the Lord gave in **John 6:28-29**.

Then they asked him, "What must we do to do the works God requires?"

Jesus answered, "The work of God is this: to believe in the one he has sent."

Here was a perfect opportunity to list all the things we have to do to meet God's requirements. Jesus could have rattled off the 10 commandments. He could have repeated the Sermon on the Mount. He could have listed any number of admonitions and restrictions necessary to achieve and maintain God's expectations of us. But what did He say? *"Believe in the one He has sent."* Period. It was a repeat of **John 3:16**, confirming that belief in the Son is the one and only requirement for salvation.

For God so loved the world that he gave his only begotten Son, that whoever believes in him shall not perish but have eternal life.

A few verses later in **John 6:38-40** He said that this wasn't just His idea, as if that wouldn't be enough, but that His Father was in complete agreement. And not only would our belief suffice to provide us with eternal life, but that it was God's will that Jesus lose none of those who believe. You and I have been known to disobey God's will, but has Jesus ever done so? And isn't He the one who's been charged with the responsibility for keeping us? Let's read it.

"For I have come down from heaven not to do my will but to do the will of him who sent me. And this is the will of him who sent me, that I shall lose none of all that he has given me, but raise them up at the last day. For my Father's will is that everyone who looks to the Son and believes in him shall have eternal life, and I will raise him up at the last day." (**John 6:38-40**)

Just in case we missed this promise, Jesus made it again even more clearly in **John 10:28-30**. *"I give them eternal life, and they shall never perish; no one can snatch them out of my hand. My Father, who has given them to me, is greater than all; no one can snatch them out of my Father's hand. I and the Father are one."* The Father and the Son have both accepted responsibility for our security. Once we're in Their hands, no one can get us away.

I have purposely only used words straight from the Lord's own mouth to make this case because I can already hear the choruses of "Yes Buts" mounting as those who refuse to take them at face value get ready to trot out their favorite verses denying Eternal Security, misinterpreted though they are.

The one characteristic of God's that gives us the most comfort is knowing that He can't lie or change His mind or contradict Himself. He can't say something in one place and then say something entirely different in another. He's consistent. If He says that we're saved solely because of our belief in Him, and that He's accepted responsibility for keeping us so, then we can count on that. As we'll see, anything in the Bible that seems to contradict these simple, straightforward statements has to be talking about something else.

But first, since He puts so much emphasis on belief, let's take a closer look at that word. What does He mean when He says "believe"? It must be more than just a casual thing because reliable statistics show, for example, that 85% of those who come forward to "receive the Lord" at a crusade or other evangelistic outreach never form any connection with a church or Bible Study or in any other way demonstrate a relationship with the Lord afterward.

And Jesus spoke of the seed that fell on rocky places. He said, *"This is the man who hears the word and at once receives it with joy. But since he has no root, he lasts only a short time. When trouble or persecution comes because of the word, he quickly falls away."* (**Matt. 13:20-21**) If these people were saved and then fell away, all His promises above have been broken. There must be more. So what does it mean to believe?

The Greek word for believe is "pistis." According the Strong's Concordance, it's a "conviction or belief respecting man's relationship to God and divine things, generally with the included idea of trust and holy fervor born of faith and joined with it." In connection with the Lord Jesus, it means "a strong and welcome conviction or belief that Jesus is the Messiah, through whom we obtain eternal salvation in the kingdom of God."

The Apostle Paul gave us valuable insight into the nature of this belief. He wrote, *If you confess with your mouth, "Jesus is Lord," and believe in your heart that God raised him from the dead, you will be saved. For it is with your heart that you believe and are justified, and it is with your mouth that you confess and are saved.* (**Romans 10:9-10**)

This isn't just some intellectual thing that carries us away on the words of a captivating speaker, only to leave us flat a short time later. It's a conviction that's formed deep in our heart, the realization that Jesus is not just a man. He's the Lord Himself, and He took upon Himself the penalty due us for our sins, which is death. And to prove that God counted His death as sufficient, He raised Jesus from the dead to be seated beside Him in the Heavenly realms. (**Ephes. 1:20**) Since God can't dwell in the presence of sin, and since the wages of sin is death, every one of our sins has to have been paid for. If even one remained unpaid, Jesus would still be in the grave. We have to believe that Jesus rose from the grave in order to believe that we will.

It's that kind of belief that gets you saved and keeps you that way, because it sets in motion a chain of events that's irreversible. There are four links in this chain. You supply two and the Lord supplies two. You hear and believe, and the Lord marks and guarantees.

And you also were included in Christ when you heard the word of truth, the gospel of your salvation. Having believed, you were marked in him with a seal, the promised Holy Spirit, who is a deposit guaranteeing our inheritance until the redemption of those who are God's possession—to the praise of his glory. (**Ephesians 1:13-14**)

The word translated "deposit" is a legal term. Today we would say Earnest Money. It's a down payment that constitutes a legal obligation to follow through with the purchase. If you've ever bought any Real Estate, you're familiar with the term. If not, here's another example. It's like we've been put on "lay away." The price has been paid and we've been taken off the display shelf until the one who has purchased us returns to claim us. In the mean time we cannot be bought by anyone else, because we legally belong to the one who has paid the deposit. *"You are not your own,"* we're told. *"You were bought with a price."* (**1 Cor. 6:19-20**)

All of this happened at our first moment of belief, before we could do anything to either earn or lose our position. The man on the cross beside Jesus is the prototype for this transaction. Having done something bad enough to get himself executed, he was promised a place in Paradise solely because he believed in his heart that Jesus was the Lord of a coming Kingdom.

Paul made it even clearer when he repeated this incredible promise in **2 Cor. 1:21-22**. *Now it is God who makes both us and you stand firm in Christ. He anointed us, set his seal of ownership on us, and put his Spirit in our hearts as a deposit, guaranteeing what is to come.*

This time He removed all doubt as to just Who it is that keeps us saved. Now it is God who makes both us and you stand firm in Christ. What could be clearer?

Union And Fellowship

If the Doctrine of Eternal Security is so clear then why all the disagreement about it? I've found two reasons. The first is the two-sided nature of our relationship with the Lord. I call one side Union. It's eternal and unconditional, based only on our belief. **Ephesians 1:13-14** describes our Union with God, sealed and guaranteed. Once we're born again, we can't become unborn. It's good forever. The Holy Spirit is sealed within us from our first moment of belief until the day of redemption.

I call the other side Fellowship and it's a bit more complicated. Fellowship is that state of continual closeness to God that enables Him to bless us in our daily lives, by making things happen for us and protecting us from attack. It's like He's teamed up with us to give us a supernatural advantage. Fellowship is defined by **1 John 1:8-9** as being both Earthly and conditional upon our behavior. Even as believers, as long as we're here on Earth we'll continue to sin. Since God can't abide in the presence of sin, our unconfessed sins interrupt our Earthly relationship with Him and could deprive us of blessings we might have otherwise received. We're still saved in the eternal sense, but out of Fellowship here on Earth.

When we're out of Fellowship, we're legitimate targets for our enemy's mischief, just like Job was. His sin was self-righteousness and because he wouldn't confess it, God had to let Satan afflict him in order to bring him to his senses. For a New Testament illustration, look at the parable of the Prodigal Son. (**Luke 15:11–32**) Like the younger son, we'll still belong to our Father's family, but won't receive any of its blessings while we're out of Fellowship. And like both Job and the Prodigal, when we return to our Father and confess our sins, we're immediately purified from all unrighteousness and restored to Fellowship.

One reason that many Christians live such defeated lives is that having only learned about the Union part of being a believer, they only know that God has forgiven their sins and that they'll go to be with Him when they die or are Raptured. They don't realize that they still need to confess every time they sin to stay in Fellowship. And so, being deprived of God's providence, they may become discouraged and even stop praying and attending church. Other believers, who don't understand the dual relationship either, look at the mess they're in and think they must have lost their salvation. Like Job's friends, they look in God's Word for confirmation, and by taking verses out of context, believe they have found the proof.

Union and Fellowship are not just New Testament ideas. In the Old Testament, even when Israel was being obedient in thought and action, doing their best to please God, the priests still had to sacrifice a lamb on the altar every morning and every evening for the sins of the people. **1 John 1:9** is the New Testament equivalent of those daily sacrifices for sin. *If we confess our sins, he is faithful and just and will forgive us our sins and purify us from all unrighteousness.* It was written for believers who are already saved, but are in danger of being out of Fellowship because of their sins.

The Gift And the Prize

The other reason people get confused is that there are two types of benefits in Eternity. The first is the free Gift called Salvation that's given to all who ask in faith irrespective of merit and guarantees our admission into the Kingdom. **Ephesians 2:8-9** is the model, saying that salvation is a Gift from God.

The second consists of Heavenly rewards we can earn for the things we do as believers here on Earth. **Philippians 3:13-14** are good verses for explaining this. *Forgetting what is behind and straining toward what is ahead, I press on toward the goal to win the prize for which God has called me heavenward in Christ Jesus.* In addition to the Gift, there's a Prize.

A gift is something given out of love, irrespective of merit, and is never taken back. A prize, on the other hand, is something we can qualify for and earn. And if we're not careful we can lose it. (**Rev. 3:11**) Paul had already received the Gift of salvation, it was behind him. Now he was focused on winning the Prize as well.

In **1 Corinthians 9:24–27** he explained the difference in greater detail. *Do you not know that in a race all the runners run, but only one gets the prize? Run in such a way as to get the prize. Everyone who competes in the games goes into strict training. They do it to get a crown that will not last; but we do it to get a crown that will last forever.*

No Olympic athlete was satisfied just to have qualified to participate in the games. Everyone wanted to win the victor's crown. Likewise, we shouldn't be satisfied just to have received the Gift of salvation. We must now live our lives as believers in such a way as to win the Prize as well.

The Bible calls some of these prizes crowns, and while the athlete's crown soon wilted away (it was a wreath of ivy) the crowns believers can win last forever. They're worth making some sacrifices for. That's why Paul said, *I beat my body and make it my slave so that after I have preached to others, I myself will not be disqualified for the prize.* (**1 Cor. 9:27**) The crowns are identified as the Everlasting Crown (Victory) in **1 Cor 9:25**, Crown of the Soul Winner in **Phil 4:1** and **1 Thes 2:19**, Crown of Righteousness in **2 Tim 4:8**, Crown of Life in **Jas 1:12** and **Rev 2:10**, and the Crown of Glory in **1 Peter 5:4**.

The difference between the Gift and the Prize is also seen in **1 Cor. 3:12-15**. *If any man builds on this foundation using gold, silver, costly stones, wood, hay or straw, his work will be shown for what it is, because the Day will bring it to light. It will be revealed with fire, and the fire will test the quality of each man's work. If what he has built survives, he will receive his reward. If it is burned up, he will suffer loss; he himself will be saved, but only as one escaping through the flames.*

At the judgment of believers, the quality of our work on earth will be tested by fire. Only work that survives the test will bring us a reward. But notice that even if all our work is destroyed in the fire, we'll still have our salvation. Why? Because it's a free Gift, given out of love, irrespective of merit.

The Lord mentioned other rewards as well. In **Matt. 6:19-21** He advised us, *"Do not store up for yourselves treasures on earth, where moth and rust destroy, and where thieves break in and steal. But store up for yourselves treasures in heaven, where moth and rust do not destroy, and where thieves do not break in and steal. For where your treasure is, there your heart will be also."*

There are things we can do as believers while here on Earth that will cause deposits to be made to our heavenly account. Some believe that this passage refers to the way we use the money we're given. Do we use it to enrich ourselves, stacking up possessions that far exceed our needs? Or do we use it to further the work of the Kingdom? Here's a hint. Our tithe is what we owe to

God. It's what we do with the money we have left after we pay it that really counts. And with the measure we use, it will be measured to us. (**Luke 6:38**)

To summarize, in the New Testament there are verses like **Ephesians 1:13-14** that talk about Union. There are verses like **1 John 1: 8-9** that talk about Fellowship. There are verses like **Ephesians 2:8-9** that talk about the Gift and there are verses like **1 Cor 9:24-27** that talk about the Prize.

Those that stress belief, explain the permanent nature of our bond with God, and are directed toward eternity are Union verses. Those that involve grace and faith are Gift verses. Those that require work and are directed at the quality of our lives on Earth are Fellowship verses, and those that require work and involve eternal rewards are Prize verses.

When you view Scripture from this perspective, all of the apparent contradictions disappear and you no longer have to wonder why God seems to be saying one thing here and something different there. The issue becomes one of correctly identifying the focal point of the particular passage you're looking at. Determine the context by reading verses around it, and assign it to one of the four categories.

Give Us An Example

Hebrews 6:4-6 is a passage often cited in opposition to Eternal Security. The entire letter is to Jewish believers who are being enticed back into keeping the Law, so the context is New Covenant vs. Old. And in verse 9 the writer hints that he's been talking about things that accompany salvation. That tells us that verses 4-6 are not about salvation but things that accompany it. More importantly the idea that a believer could do something to irretrievably lose his salvation is in direct contradiction to the very clear promise that the Holy Spirit is sealed within us from the very first moment of belief until the day of redemption.

So what could these believers be in danger of falling away from due to their sins? Fellowship. And what could prevent them from being restored? The practice of Old Covenant remedies for sin rather than invoking **1 John 1:9**. They'd be relegating the death of the Lord to the same status as that of the twice-daily lamb that was the Old Testament sacrifice for sin. The Law was only a shadow of the good things to come, not the realities themselves. Once the Reality appeared, the shadow was no longer effective. And what would be their penalty? Living a defeated life, bearing no fruit, all their works burned in the judgment of **1 Cor. 3**. But still saved? Yes. **Hebrews 6:4-6** is a Fellowship passage.

Suppose There Is No Security?

In closing, let's look at the alternative. What are we faced with? If **Hebrews 6:4-6** for example applies to our salvation then if we ever sin after being saved we'll be lost forever with no way back, because the Lord would have to be crucified all over again to retrieve us. The New Covenant would be worse than the Old, not better. They were condemned for their actions. But according to **Matt. 5** we'd be condemned for our thoughts. They couldn't murder. We can't even be angry. They couldn't commit adultery. We can't even have a lustful thought. Think of it. No anger, ever. No lust, ever. No envy, ever. No idolatry, ever. No favoritism or discrimination, ever. No impure thoughts or deeds of any kind, ever. Is this the Good News, the incomparable riches of His Grace? Did God become man and die the most painful death ever devised only to put His children into an even more untenable position than before? Are we saved by grace only to be placed under the constraints of an even more severely administered law? I can't believe so.

Some take a more moderate view of this saying that God would never take back the gift of salvation, but that we can return it. To justify this position they have to put words in the Lord's mouth. When He says in **John 10:28**, "No one can snatch them out of my hand," they have to insert the phrase "but us" after "no one". Same with **Romans 8:38-39**.

For I am convinced that neither death nor life, neither angels nor demons, neither the present nor the future, nor any powers, neither height nor depth, nor anything else in all creation, will be able to separate us from the love of God that is in Christ Jesus our Lord. They have to insert the phrase "but us" after "in all creation".

None of this defense of Eternal Security is intended to condone sin. As an indication of our gratitude for the gift of salvation, believers are continually admonished in Scripture to live our lives in a manner pleasing to God. Not to earn or keep it, but to thank the Lord for giving it to us. And to help us do that, the Holy Spirit has come to dwell in us to guide and direct us, and to pray for us. Since the Spirit of God lives in us we are no longer controlled by the sin nature and can choose to please God by the way we live. And even though we do this out of gratitude for the Gift He's already given, which is Union with Him, He blesses us both here on Earth (Fellowship) and in Eternity (the Prize).

5. O You Of Little Faith

A Bible Study by Jack Kelley

Increase Our Faith

Jesus left there and went to his hometown, accompanied by his disciples. When the Sabbath came, he began to teach in the synagogue, and many who heard him were amazed.

"Where did this man get these things?" they asked. "What's this wisdom that has been given him, that he even does miracles! Isn't this the carpenter? Isn't this Mary's son and the brother of James, Joseph, Judas and Simon? Aren't his sisters here with us?" And they took offense at him.

Jesus said to them, "Only in his hometown, among his relatives and in his own house is a prophet without honor." He could not do any miracles there, except lay his hands on a few sick people and heal them. And he was amazed at their lack of faith. (**Mark 6:1-6**)

Of all the miraculous works of God, it seems like healing is the most impressive to us. We pray for a favorable outcome to some crisis real or imagined, and when we get it we think it might have been just a coincidence. The weather changes for the better before an important event, money arrives in the mail just in time, an adversary is suddenly accommodating, a parking place opens up where there was none, someone else is heavily favored for the promotion but it goes to us. All these leave room for "good fortune" or personal credit. But when a sick person is suddenly well, it could only be God.

Perhaps it's because in many (dare I say most?) parts of the Church supernatural healing is so rare. Most of what we know about them is polluted by the quacks on cable TV to the point where many people dismiss the idea out of hand. On the rare occasion when we become convinced of a legitimate healing we stand in awe of the faith it must have required.

It Wasn't Always That Way

Back in the Lord's day people were apparently used to that sort of thing. What got their attention was when the blind were given sight, twisted crippled limbs were made straight and fully functional, or the dead were raised to life. The **Mark 6** passage above is a case in point. Because the people of the Lord's home town had known Him from childhood, their faith in His supernatural power was weak, so weak in fact that "all" He could do was heal a few sick people. No "real" miracles for the people of Nazareth!

All through His ministry, wherever He went people without number were healed. They followed Him on foot for days, sometimes winding up 50-60 miles from home without food or shelter. On two occasions that we know of He fed them Himself because there wasn't anything for them to eat. Another miracle! When people heard He was coming to their town they brought their sick into the square where they waited, expecting to be healed. When He sent the disciples out the same things happened through them. By the thousands people were healed.

They believed it, they expected it, they experienced it. Supernatural healing was such an everyday experience that when He couldn't do it, their lack of faith amazed Him. Look at these examples.

Jesus went throughout Galilee, teaching in their synagogues, preaching the good news of the kingdom, and healing every disease and sickness among the people. News about him spread all over Syria, and people brought to him all who were ill with various diseases, those suffering severe pain, the demon-possessed, those having seizures, and the paralyzed, and he healed them. Large crowds from Galilee, the Decapolis, Jerusalem, Judea and the region across the Jordan followed him. (**Matt. 4:23–25**)

*When they had crossed over, they landed at Gennesaret. And when the men of that place recognized Jesus, they sent word to all the surrounding country. People brought all their sick to him and begged him to let the sick just touch the edge of his cloak, and all who touched him were healed. (***Matt. 13:34–36***)*

And it wasn't just Jesus. He gave this healing power to His disciples, too, to show us that He could work these miracles through men of faith.

Then Jesus went around teaching from village to village. Calling the Twelve to him, he sent them out two by two and gave them authority over evil spirits. They went out and preached that people should repent. They drove out many demons and anointed many sick people with oil and healed them. (**Mark 6:6–7, 12–13**)

As a result, people brought the sick into the streets and laid them on beds and mats so that at least Peter's shadow might fall on some of them as he passed by. Crowds gathered also from the towns around Jerusalem, bringing their sick and those tormented by evil spirits, and all of them were healed. (**Acts 5:15-16**)

God did extraordinary miracles through Paul, so that even handkerchiefs and aprons that had touched him were taken to the sick, and their illnesses were cured and the evil spirits left them. (**Acts 19:11-12**)

Things sure are different today. Now when our prayers aren't answered, we either make excuses for God (it wasn't His will or it wasn't His timing) or we blame Him (He doesn't heal people any more). Why don't we ever place the responsibility with us? **Hebrews 13:8** says that Jesus Christ is the same yesterday today and forever and yet our experiences are different from those of the first believers. If He's the same then we, the believers, must be different.

No where in the Gospels, when asked to heal someone, did Jesus say, "It's not God's timing." The one time a man asked him if He was willing, Jesus replied, "I am willing." (**Matt. 8:2-3**) The one time a man asked If He was able, Jesus replied, "If you believe, I am able." (**Mark 9:23**) The one time a man's friends tried to convince him it was too late, because his daughter had died, Jesus said, "Don't be afraid, just believe and she will be healed." (**Luke 8:50**).

In Lystra there sat a man crippled in his feet, who was lame from birth and had never walked. He listened to Paul as he was speaking. Paul looked directly at him, saw that he had faith to be healed and called out, "Stand up on your feet!" At that, the man jumped up and began to walk. (**Acts 14:8-10**)

And as for the opinion that healing (and other Spiritual Gifts) were only for the 1st Century Church to help stimulate membership, there isn't a single verse in the New Testament to support such a claim. The fact that there are documented cases of supernatural healing today puts that argument to naught.

I've told the story before about a woman with epilepsy who came to our church one Sunday morning. In the middle of the message she keeled over with a seizure right in front of everyone. I called some people up to help me pray over her and she was healed then and there. After her doctor confirmed it she threw away her medicine and has never had another seizure. She told me she had seen everything in a dream before it happened and although she hadn't attended our church before, she believed that if she came she would he healed. She had the faith to walk into that strange congregation knowing that she might make a complete fool of herself, but believing that God would heal her. He did. *He said to her, "Daughter, your faith has healed you. Go in peace and be freed from your suffering."* (**Mark 5:34**)

When you net out the duplicate accounts, some variation of that phrase appears seven times in the Gospels. Seven times, He credited the person's faith for their healing. Seven is the number of divine completion. He knows that His power to heal is constant. The variable is our faith.

This has led me to conclude that a miraculous event is simply the intersection of God's constant power with the faith of a believer.

Faith comes from hearing the message, and the message is heard through the word of Christ. (**Romans 10:17**)

Life was so much more tenuous in Biblical times than in ours that we can't begin to imagine the difference. Nor can we understand how much closer to God they were. Their faith was real, the most critical component of their life. Those who could, read the Bible. Those who couldn't, listened to those who could. Their lives centered around the study of His word. There wasn't any entertainment industry so they told the stories of Biblical heroes to their children. They discussed theology with each other. Every male from the age of 12 knew the Torah by heart. All this was done in obedience to God's word.

Hear, O Israel: The LORD our God, the LORD is one. Love the LORD your God with all your heart and with all your soul and with all your strength. These commandments that I give you today are to be upon your hearts. Impress them on your children. Talk about them when you sit at home and when you walk along the road, when you lie down and when you get up. Tie them as symbols on your hands and bind them on your foreheads. Write them on the doorframes of your houses and on your gates. (**Deut. 6:4-9**)

There were no drug companies and no hospitals. Their doctors were the priests. God promised them that if they obeyed His commandments He would see to it that they wouldn't get the diseases of the Egyptians. (**Exodus 15:26**) God was their healer, and when they were obedient, they enjoyed healthy secure lives equal to or longer than ours, and every bit as satisfying. It was preventive medicine in its purest form.

All these blessings will come upon you and accompany you if you obey the LORD your God: You will be blessed in the city and blessed in the country. The fruit of your womb will be blessed, and the crops of your land and the young of your livestock-the calves of your herds and the lambs of your flocks. Your basket and your kneading trough will be blessed. You will be blessed when you come in and blessed when you go out. The LORD will grant that the enemies who rise up against you will be defeated before you. They will come at you from one direction but flee from you in seven. The LORD will send a blessing on your barns and on everything you put your hand to. The LORD your God will bless you in the land he is giving you. (**Deut. 28:2-8**)

A Tale Of Two Stories

The story of the Old Testament is one of obedience. In fact you can summarize the entire Old Testament in one question from God. "Israel, are you going to obey me or not?" By obeying His commandments they lived worry free lives, ate healthy food, lived long and prosperous lives. When they got off the track, their lives fell apart. Time after time they repeated the cycle of obedience and blessing followed by disobedience and cursing. And then, to their great shame, their final answer to God was, "No."

Some Christians, having studied the history of Israel, try to recreate their society of blessing by obeying the commandments. They don't understand that the story of the New Testament is one of faith. It can be summarized by a single question too, but now God is asking us, "Church, are you going to believe me or not?

Several times I have written of the Lord's promise to meet all of our needs if we'll just seek His Kingdom and His righteousness (**Matt. 6:31-33**). These are both imputed to us by faith. We're not to worry about our lives here because the Lord has sworn to provide for us. Our job is to trust Him. Even in times of trial we're to walk by faith, not by sight (**2 Cor. 5:7**). Paul admonished us not to focus on the things that can be seen because they're temporary. We're to fix our eyes on the things that can't be seen because they're eternal. (**2 Cor. 4:18)** God will take care of the rest. Here are some examples.

Are you feeling down trodden or discouraged? Overcome by the worries of life?

Rejoice in the Lord always. I will say it again: Rejoice! Let your gentleness be evident to all. The Lord is near. Do not be anxious about anything, but in everything, by prayer and petition, with thanksgiving, present your requests to God. And the peace of God, which transcends all understanding, will guard your hearts and your minds in Christ Jesus. And my God will meet all your needs according to his glorious riches in Christ Jesus. (**Phil 4:4-7, 19**) Rejoice in faith.

Do you carry a burden of guilt because of your sins?

If we confess our sins, he is faithful and just and will forgive us our sins and purify us from all unrighteousness. (**1 John 1:9**) Confess in faith.

Do you have money problems?

Give, and it will be given to you. A good measure, pressed down, shaken together and running over, will be poured into your lap. For with the measure you use, it will be measured to you." (**Luke 6:38**) Give in faith.

Or health problems?

Is any one of you sick? He should call the elders of the church to pray over him and anoint him with oil in the name of the Lord. And the prayer offered in faith will make the sick person well; the Lord will raise him up. If he has sinned, he will be forgiven. Therefore confess your sins to each other and pray for each other so that you may be healed. The prayer of a righteous man is powerful and effective. (**James 5:14–16**) Pray in faith.

For the most part we ignore these admonitions. As a result we live lives filled with stress and worry because we spend more than we earn. Our food and drink poison us so we pay outrageous health care costs. Our medical profession practices corrective medicine because doctors only prosper when their patients are sick. Our hospitals are a leading cause of death, second only to the heart problems caused by our lifestyle and diet. Most of us are only 2 major illnesses away from financial ruin, and after untold trillions of dollars spent on research and 3000 years of experimentation, our lives are neither longer nor more satisfying than the Jews of David and Solomon's day.

Israel was required to obey God's commandments to enjoy health and prosperity. The Church is called to believe His promises. At this point in time it looks like we're not doing any better at our job than they did at theirs. Unless we correct that there's no way we can prepare for the days ahead. As the apostles said to the Lord, our prayer should also be, "Increase our faith!"

6. From This Day On I Will Bless You

On the twenty-fourth day of the ninth month, in the second year of Darius, the word of the LORD came to the prophet Haggai: "This is what the LORD Almighty says: 'Ask the priests what the law says: If a person carries consecrated meat in the fold of his garment, and that fold touches some bread or stew, some wine, oil or other food, does it become consecrated?' " The priests answered, "No."

Then Haggai said, "If a person defiled by contact with a dead body touches one of these things, does it become defiled?"

"Yes," the priests replied, "it becomes defiled." Then Haggai said, " 'So it is with this people and this nation in my sight,' declares the LORD. 'Whatever they do and whatever they offer there is defiled.

" 'Now give careful thought to this from this day on —consider how things were before one stone was laid on another in the LORD's temple. When anyone came to a heap of twenty measures, there were only ten. When anyone went to a wine vat to draw fifty measures, there were only twenty. I struck all the work of your hands with blight, mildew and hail, yet you did not turn to me,' declares the LORD.

'From this day on, from this twenty-fourth day of the ninth month, give careful thought to the day when the foundation of the LORD's temple was laid. Give careful thought: Is there yet any seed left in the barn? Until now, the vine and the fig tree, the pomegranate and the olive tree have not borne fruit. " 'From this day on I will bless you.' " (**Haggai 2:10-19**)

After returning from the Babylonian captivity the Jews had faced a lot of resistance in trying to rebuild their Temple. Finally they gave up, wrongly deciding that perhaps it wasn't God's timing. When they did, they faced another kind of trouble as well. They lost the Lord's favor, and from then on no matter how hard they worked they weren't successful. Each time they thought they were getting ahead, they discovered they were actually getting behind. Even their offerings weren't pleasing to Him.

On the day they they turned back to the construction of the Lord's house, this all stopped and He restored their blessings. What was the lesson? He wanted them to put His house first, especially in times of persecution.

Financial Disasters

The Lord's depletion of their stored up goods is a model of today's losses, first in the decline of the dollar and now in the decline of property values. The dollar has lost much of it's previous value in the world markets, making the foreign made products we buy, or those made of imported materials, more expensive. (Try to find something on your shopping list that doesn't fit into one or the other of those two categories.)

The average home in the US is now worth about 25% less than it was a few years ago. Since most people didn't have 25% equity in their homes to begin with, that means the average home owner now owes more on his or her property can it can be sold for. Estimated losses for the Real Estate market will exceed $1 trillion. Officials are projecting that well over 1,000 banks will fail before this financial crisis is over. If they're right then one out of every eight banks is already in some kind of financial trouble. Retired Fed Chairman Alan Greenspan called this situation a "once-in-a-century" financial disaster, and it's impacting financial markets all over the world.

Natural Disasters

The blight, mildew, and hail of **Haggai 2** are models of the natural disasters that are also afflicting us now. As it was with the Israelites, the fruits of our labors are disappearing, and our offerings are not pleasing to the Lord.

Things that were external and physical in the Old Testament often become internal and spiritual in the New. In the Old Testament the Temple was a building in Jerusalem, but in the New Testament we are the Temple of God (**1 Cor. 3:16**) and things aren't national anymore, they're personal. The good news is that as believers we're not held captive to the fate of our nation like the Israelites were. In **2 Chron. 7:14** the Lord promised the Israelites,

If my people, who are called by my name, will humble themselves and pray and seek my face and turn from their wicked ways, then will I hear from heaven and will forgive their sin and will heal their land.

This was a promise to the Jewish people that if as a nation they would return to their covenant relationship with God he would restore His blessings on the Promised

Land. The New Testament application of this promise for the Church can be found in **Matt. 6:31-33**.

So do not worry, saying, 'What shall we eat?' or 'What shall we drink?' or 'What shall we wear?' For the pagans run after all these things, and your heavenly Father knows that you need them. But seek first his kingdom and his righteousness, and all these things will be given to you as well.

This is a promise to each of us personally. We're not to worry about how we'll get by. We're to seek first His Kingdom and His righteousness and all these things will be given us as well. The Lord's feeding of first 5,000 and then 4,000 was meant to teach us that He is able to provide for us when we're willing to let Him. The feeding of 5,000 is the only one of His many pre-resurrection miracles that's described in all four gospels, which means that except for the Resurrection it was His most important one.

Now that doesn't mean we can sit back like baby birds with our mouths open crying, "Feed me". Paul said that he who will not work shall not eat. (**2 Thes. 3:10**) But it does mean that we are to put our trust in Him to take care of us regardless of the circumstances, and to do the work He gives us no matter what it is, and concentrate on coming closer to Him.

Let's Get Personal

The time is coming soon when every Christian family in America will either have a personal experience of miraculous survival in the face of financial disaster or will know of one who has. In each case the story will be the same as it was for the Jews of Haggai's day. As soon as they stopped worrying about their own lives and turned back to the business of building the Lord's Temple, His blessings were restored. As soon as we stop worrying about how we're going to survive the potentially difficult days ahead and focus our lives on Him we'll experience the same result.

Please don't misunderstand me here. I'm not talking about some external application of legalism. I'm not talking about mindless obedience to rules and commandments while our hearts are in rebellion . I'm talking about an inner reliance on the Lord, about restoring our faith in both His ability and His desire to provide for us.

There's no prophecy we can point to for assurance that the Lord will save the United States. Applying Old Testament promises meant for Israel to the US is just another form of replacement theology. This is not a national issue. This is a personal one, and each one of us will determine the outcome for our own lives.

The very day that Israel decided to resume building the Lord's House He restored their blessings. This is a part of the prophecy you can claim for yourself. The very day you determine in your heart to place your life in His hands He will begin blessing you.

I have come that they may have life, and have it to the full (**John 10:10**). *You will be made rich in every way so that you can be* *generous on every occasion, and through us your generosity will result in thanksgiving to God* (**2 Cor. 9:11**)

That doesn't necessarily mean we'll all get to keep everything we now have. Some of our possessions are actually the cause of our problems, both because we've over spent to get them and because they've taken our focus off the Lord. Some of them have even enslaved us, and were much more fun in the getting than they are in the having. Many came with ongoing ownership costs like interest or other fees that eat away at our resources.

The Lord will show you what, if anything, has to go. And don't worry about incurring losses. If He tells you to get rid of something and you obey, then over time He'll restore your losses. How do I know this? Three reasons. One, He wants you to store up treasure in Heaven (**Matt. 6:19-21**). Two, He's promised that if you follow His direction you'll be made rich in every way so you can be generous on every occasion (**2 Cor. 9:11**). You can't do either of these if you're taking huge losses. Three, He promised to repay you for the years the locusts have eaten. (**Joel 2:25**) That means when you turn back to Him He'll give you joy in return for the misery you've caused yourself.

Give, and it will be given to you. A good measure, pressed down, shaken together and running over, will be poured into your lap. For with the measure you use, it will be measured to you (**Luke 6:38**).

But don't think He'll restore your fortunes just so you can keep all your toys, or get them all back. That's the failure of the so-called prosperity gospel. The Lord's promise is that we'll be made rich so we can be generous, not so we can be irresponsible or selfish. It's in being generous that we store up treasure in Heaven, where no form of property or currency devaluation can do us harm. Generous people are also the happiest people. See how it works?

Some will say, "I'm so far in debt even if I started today it would take 10 years to get out." I say, "How much debt will you have in 10 years if you don't start today?" The way I see things shaping up, you can either downsize voluntarily and do it the easy way, or you can wait till you're forced to and do it the hard way.

Now I know better than anyone that the rapture could come any day now and spare us all these things. But if you're part of the 90% of believers with a pagan world view, the longer He waits the more time you'll have to finally start storing up treasure in Heaven, where it will benefit you forever. When you know you're moving to a different city soon, you begin thinking about your new home and what your life will be like there. Take my word for it, you're moving to a different city soon, so you'd better start thinking about it.

I used to pray for more money so I could pay the bills on my outrageous lifestyle. I didn't get it. Now I live on less than 1/3 of what I used to spend and in every sense I'm wealthier than I was. Now I pray for more money so I can give more to His work, and He always sends it. You think maybe there's a lesson in there somewhere?

7. The Pre-Tribulation Rapture Of The Church

A Bible Study by Jack Kelley

Some body once asked me a great question on the rapture of the Church. "Does Scripture actually promise a Pre-Tribulation Rapture, or is it just an opinion passed along from teacher to student?" Then he challenged me to cite even one Bible verse that would lead a person to believe the Pre-Trib position if they hadn't already heard about it from some Bible teacher. He said that in all his studies he's not been able to find one. Let's see if he's right.

First, Some General Points

The Rapture is not another name for the Second Coming. As **1 Thes. 4:15-17** and **John 14:1-3** explain, the Rapture is an unscheduled secret event where Jesus comes part way to Earth to meet His Church in the air and take us to be with Him where He now is. I say unscheduled and secret because its specific timing will remain unknown until it actually happens.

On the other hand, The Second Coming is a scheduled public event where Jesus comes all the way to Earth with His Church to establish a Kingdom here. I say scheduled and public because the general time of His coming will be known on Earth over 3 1/2 years in advance, and public because everyone on Earth will be able to witness His arrival. **Matt. 24:29-30** says it will happen shortly after the Great Tribulation has ended and all the nations will see the Son of Man coming on the clouds in the sky.

Membership in the Church and therefore participation in the Rapture is contingent upon having personally accepted the Lord's death as payment in full for your sins. While His death actually purchased full pardons for everyone, we each have to personally ask to have ours activated. Everyone who asks for salvation receives an unconditional, irrevocable "Yes!" (**Matt. 7:7-8, John 3:16, Ephes. 1:13-14**) *For no matter how many promises God has made, they are "Yes" in Christ.* (**2 Corinth. 1:20**)

It's Greek To Me

And finally, although cynics can truthfully say that the word Rapture doesn't appear in any passage of Scripture, the statement is not correct in its intent. Rapture is a word of Latin origin, not Hebrew or Greek, the languages of the Bible. (One of the earliest translations of the Bible was into Latin, and the word rapture comes from there.) Its Greek equivalent is *harpazo*, which is found in the Greek text of **1 Thes. 4:17**. When they're translated into English, both words mean "to be caught up, or snatched away." *Harpazo*, the word Paul actually used, comes from roots that mean, "to raise from the ground" and" take for oneself" and hints that in doing so the Lord is eagerly claiming us for Himself.

So while the Latin word doesn't appear in our Bibles, the event it describes certainly does. There's a similar situation with the word Lucifer, also of Latin origin. It doesn't appear in any of the original texts either, but no one would be naive enough to deny the existence of Satan on such a flimsy basis. With that introduction, let's go first to the best known of the Rapture passages.

According to the Lord's own word, we tell you that we who are still alive, who are left till the coming of the Lord, will certainly not precede those who have fallen asleep. For the Lord himself will come down from heaven, with a loud command, with the voice of the archangel and with the trumpet call of God, and the dead in Christ will rise first. After that, we who are still alive and are left will be caught up together with them in the clouds to meet the Lord in the air. And so we will be with the Lord forever. (**1 Thes. 4:15-17**)

Most of us are very familiar with these verses. But notice they don't tell you when the rapture happens, only that it does. Notice also that the Lord doesn't come all the way to Earth. We meet Him in the clouds and then according to **John 14:1-3** go back with Him to where He came from. If this was the 2nd coming, He would be coming here to be where we are, not coming to take us there to be where He is. Paul described the same event in **1 Cor 15:51-52**. In a flash, in the twinkling of an eye the dead in Christ will rise and the living will be transformed. There he said that he was disclosing a secret, but the resurrection of the dead was not a secret. It can be found through out the Old Testament. The secret was that some would not die, but would be taken alive into the Lord's presence following an instantaneous transformation. The rapture happens fast. In one instant we're walking on Earth and in the very next, we're in the Kingdom.

By the way, don't try to use the trumpet reference in verse 52 to pin the timing of the rapture to some other event. Since both the Corinthian passage and the one from Thessalonians describe the same things, it's safe to assume that the term last trump refers to the fact that the trumpet call of God from **1 Thes. 4:16** will signal the end of the Church Age, at which time the Church will disappear from Earth. So these two references both say that one generation of humans won't die but will be suddenly changed from our earthly form to our heavenly one. And since both **Matt. 24:31** (*they'll gather His elect from one end of the heavens to the other*) and **Rev. 17:14** (*with Him will be His called, chosen, and faithful followers*) say that we'll be with the Lord when He returns, this has to happen sometime before the 2nd Coming. And it can't be just the resurrected believers coming back with Him because the Rapture passages above say that we'll be changed at the same time as the dead are raised.

So When Does This Happen?

In the New Testament, the clearest indication we get in the timing department is found in **1 Thes. 1:9-10**. *They tell how you turned to God from idols to serve the living and true God, and to wait for his Son from heaven, whom he raised from the dead—Jesus, who rescues us from the coming wrath.*

The Greek word translated "from" in this passage is *"apo."* Translated literally, it means we'll be rescued from the time, the place, or any relation to God's wrath. It denotes both departure and separation. This is supported by **1**

Thes. 5:9 that declares, *"God did not appoint us to suffer wrath but to receive salvation through our Lord Jesus Christ."*

Some folks are fond of pointing out that you can't use God's wrath interchangeably with the Great Tribulation. They're not the same, they say. And they're right, the two terms are not synonymous. The Great Tribulation is 3 1/2 years long and begins in **Rev. 11-13**. God's wrath is much longer, beginning in **Rev. 6**, as verse 17 explains. Some try to deny this but the Scripture is clear. The time of God's wrath begins with the Seal Judgments. The Bowl Judgments that come later don't begin the time of His wrath, they conclude it. (**Rev. 15:1**) Being rescued from the time, the place and any relation to God's Wrath means the Church has to disappear before **Rev. 6**, and that's why we believe the Rapture takes place in **Rev. 4** and the Church is the group of believers in view in heaven in **Rev. 5**.

You Be The Judge

Now let's apply my questioner's litmus test. Could a believer, sitting alone on the proverbial desert isle with nothing but a Bible and with no pre-conceived ideas, conclude that there's a pre-trib Rapture just from reading about it, or could he only be led into this position by first hearing someone teach him about it? Well, From **Isaiah 13:9-13** and **Amos 5:18-20**, he would have learned that God is going to judge the Earth for it's sins in a terrible time called the Day of the Lord when He'll pour out His wrath on mankind. Reading **Matt. 24:21-22** would have told him that this time of judgment would be so bad that if the Lord didn't put a stop to it no one would survive. But the Lord will put a stop to it by returning in power and glory. Since he would know that the Lord hasn't returned yet, he would know that God's wrath is still in the future.

When he got to **1 Thes. 1:9-10** he would see a pretty clear statement. Jesus rescues us from the coming wrath. In the "who, what, where, when, and why" methodology of the investigative reporter he would have the Who, (Jesus) the what, (rescues us) and the when (the time of the coming wrath). Reading on he would come to **1 Thes. 4:15:17** and get the where (from Earth to the clouds) and in **1 Thes. 5:9** the why (because we're not appointed to wrath). From there he would logically conclude that since we'll be rescued around the time of the coming wrath and since we're not appointed to wrath, our rescue has to precede it.

He could also answer another of the investigative reporter's questions in **1 Thes. 4:15:17** and that's how it would happen. The Lord himself will come down from Heaven into our atmosphere and suddenly snatch us away from Earth to join Him there. In chapter 5 he would learn that he would never know the exact timing of this event but only that it would precede the coming wrath. Of course there are many more passages I could reference but I think I've made my point and answered the question. In fact I'll go one step further.

I believe that since our hypothetical reader has no one to persuade him differently, he would assume that what he's reading is to be taken literally. And if that's the case, then the pre-trib position is the only conclusion he could logically come to, because every other position requires a moderate to massive re-interpretation of Scripture. I contend that left alone to work this out with only the Holy Spirit as his guide he would expect to be raptured before the wrath of God begins in **Rev. 6**. You see, God didn't write the Bible to confuse us, but to inform us. It's mankind that's gotten everything all mixed up. If you give the Holy Spirit a clear minded student, uncontaminated by man's opinions and prejudices, He would bring that person to the understanding of the rapture that's most consistent with a literal interpretation of Scripture. And that requires a pre-trib rapture.

But Wait, There's More

While we're on the topic, there's another issue that points to a pre-trib Rapture and it comes to us in the form of a clue in **1 Thes. 4:15**, right at the beginning of the Rapture passage. Verse 15 opens with the phrase *"According to the Lord's own word."* There simply is no place in the New Testament where Jesus speaks of some being resurrected and some others being transformed to meet the Lord in the air. He never said anything like that, nor does he even imply such a thing. Those who believe they see it in **Matt. 24:40-41** first have to ignore the fact that Jesus was explaining events on Earth on the actual day of His return, which would place the Rapture after the

2nd Coming, something no one believes. They also have to ignore the fact that in **Matt. 24:40-41** both believers and non-believers are sent somewhere, believers being received unto Him, while non-believers are sent away. You have to research the Greek words translated "taken" (*paralambano*) and "left" (*alphiemi*) to realize this, but when you do you'll see that the English is misleading. No Rapture view includes the disposition of non-believers, nor does it even mention them.

By the way, this is a great example of why the literal, historical, grammatical interpretation is so important. Our Bible was mostly written in Hebrew and Greek. Every translation relies on the movement of words from one language to another. This process doesn't always produce a perfect fit, and so learned men have to make allowances for this and exercise their own judgment from time to time. But men are not perfect. We all have our biases. When it's an important issue where you want an exact meaning it's always a good idea to double-check their work. Fortunately we have an incredible tool in the Strong's Concordance. It contains every Hebrew and Greek word in the Bible with their primary and secondary meanings, how often each word appears in the Bible and what meanings are used in each appearance. You can compare these with the meaning the translators used and see if you agree with their treatment of the passage. By doing this with **Matt. 24:40-41**, you'll find that the primary meaning of paralambano is to receive and the primary meaning of alphiemi is to send away. People with a post-trib disposition read **1 Thes. 4:15**, and then turned to **Matt. 24:40–41** where they saw one group being "taken" and another group being "left" after the end of the Great Tribulation. Assuming that these were the Lord's own words Paul was referring to, they stopped there. They had seen what they wanted to see.

In actuality **Matt. 24:40–41** is most likely a preview of the Sheep and Goat judgment of Tribulation survivors. The word taken (received) refers to believers going live into the Kingdom, and the word left (sent away) applies to non-believers who are sent to the place prepared for the Devil and his angels. (**Matt 25:31–46**) Of course none of this pertains to our desert island reader above. The verses I used there are clear enough that they don't require any research into the original language. So he wouldn't need a Strong's Concordance, just his Bible.

What's Your Point?

So if Jesus never taught about the Rapture, to which of the "Lord's own words" was Paul referring? Some dismiss the phrase, saying that Paul was speaking of a conversation he had with the Lord that doesn't appear in Scripture. But I think we deserve a better answer than that. Remember, 1st Thessalonians was probably Paul's first written communication, undertaken in 51AD. Depending on whose opinion you accept, Matthew's Gospel was either just being written or was still nearly 10 years away. Those who give it an early date say it was written to the Jews in Jerusalem and may even have been written in Hebrew. In any case neither it nor any other Gospel was yet in wide distribution. (Mark's Gospel, the other candidate for earliest one written, doesn't contain an equivalent to **Matt 24:40-41**.) So if Paul was referring to Scripture, as I believe he was, it had to be the Old Testament. Yes, like everything else in God's plan, you'll find hints of the Rapture even in the Old Testament.

Look at this passage from **Isaiah 26:19-21**. *But your dead will live; their bodies will rise. You who dwell in the dust, wake up and shout for joy. Your dew is like the dew of the morning; the earth will give birth to her dead. Go, my people, enter your rooms and shut the doors behind you; hide yourselves for a little while until his wrath has passed by. See, the LORD is coming out of his dwelling to punish the people of the earth for their sins.*

Notice how the pronouns change from second person when God speaks of His people to third person when He speaks of the people of the Earth. It means the two groups are different. Those called "my people" are told to "enter your rooms" (the rooms of **John 14:1-3**?) because the others, called "the people of Earth" are going to be punished for their sins in a period of time called His Wrath. Sound familiar? (Note: the Hebrew word translated "go" in the phrase "Go my people" is translated "come" in some translations, recalling the command to John in **Revelation 4**, "Come up here!" But the word has another primary meaning and it's my favorite. It means vanish. "Vanish, my people!" Yes we will.)

Not by any stretch of the imagination has this passage

been literally fulfilled. It's an End Times prophecy that promises a resurrection of the dead and hiding of God's people while His Wrath is unleashed on the people of Earth for their sins. And it was written 2750 years ago. The hiding of the Jews in the desert on Earth at the beginning of the Great Tribulation (**Rev. 12:14**) cannot be considered as a fulfillment of this passage because no resurrection accompanies it. (The resurrection of Old Testament believers takes place at the end of the Great Tribulation. (**Daniel 12:2**)) Of course, no one knows for sure that this is the passage Paul referred to, but as evidence of its influence on him, let's compare it with what Paul wrote in **1 Thessalonians 4-5**.

Isaiah : *But your dead will live; their bodies will rise. You who dwell in the dust, wake up and shout for joy. Your dew is like the dew of the morning; the earth will give birth to her dead.*

Paul: *The dead in Christ will rise first .*

Isaiah : *Go, my people, enter your rooms and shut the doors behind you; hide yourselves for a little while until his wrath has passed by.*

Paul: *After that, we who are still alive and are left will be caught up together with them in the clouds to meet the Lord in the air.*

Isaiah : *See, the LORD is coming out of his dwelling to punish the people of the earth for their sins.*

Paul: *While people are saying, "Peace and safety," destruction will come on them suddenly, as labor pains on a pregnant woman, and they will not escape.*

The wording is a little different, but it sure looks to me like they're describing the same event.

And Still More

There are other sound theological reasons why the Church will be raptured before the End Times judgments begin. One is that the Lord seems to keep Israel and the Church separate, never dealing with both at the same time (**Acts 15: 13-18**) If the primary purpose of Daniel's 70th week is to finish fulfilling the six promises to Israel in **Daniel 9:24**, then the Church has to disappear before it begins.

Another is that the Church was purified at the cross at which time all the punishment due us was born by the Lord Himself. From that time forward the Church is considered by God to be as righteous as He is (**2 Cor 5:17 & 21**) The idea that the Church needs to undergo some discipline to become worthy to dwell with God is not scriptural and denies the Lord's completed work on the cross.

And third, the stated purpose of the Great Tribulation is twofold, to purify Israel and completely destroy the unbelieving nations. (**Jeremiah 30:1-11**) The Church isn't destined for either of these outcomes. There are also several subtle clues that on their own can't be used to support the pre-trib position, but which underscore the validity of the clear passages I've just cited. Take for instance the fact that Enoch, who bears a great similarity to the Church, disappeared before the Great Flood, that the angels couldn't destroy Sodom and Gomorrah until

Lot and his family were clear, and that Daniel was missing from the story of the fiery furnace, a model of the Great Tribulation.

When the Lord described His coming in **Luke 17:26-29** He said that it would be both like the days of Noah (some will be preserved through the accompanying judgments) and the days of Lot (some will taken away before them). And what about the promise He made to the Church in Philadelphia that he would keep us out of the "hour" of trial coming on the whole world. (**Rev. 3:10**)

But being asked to cite verses that didn't require any prior knowledge I picked two that are clearest to me, **1 Thes. 1:9-10** and **Isaiah 26: 19-21**. And so by the testimony of two witnesses, one in the Old Testament and one in the New, we see the physical separation of believers from non-believers preceding the time of Judgment. And by the testimony of two witnesses a thing shall be established. (**Deut. 19:15**) Of course some won't be convinced until we show them a verse that says the rapture will precede the Great Tribulation in those exact words. Obviously, such a verse doesn't exist. I guess we'll just have to wait and explain it to them on the way up.

8. Daniel's 70 Weeks Prophecy

A Bible Study by Jack Kelley

Many believe that **Daniel 9:24-27** is the most important passage of prophecy in all of Scripture. Almost every mistake I've run across in studying the various interpretations of End Times Prophecy can be traced back to a misunderstanding of this passage.

Before plowing into it we'll back up a little and review the context. Daniel was an old man, probably in his eighties. He'd been in Babylon for nearly 70 years and knew from reading the recently completed scroll of Jeremiah's writings (specifically the part we know as **Jeremiah 25:8-11**) that the 70-year captivity God had ordained for Israel was just about over (**Daniel 9:2**).

The reason for the captivity had been Israel's insistence upon worshiping the false gods of their pagan neighbors. Its duration of 70 years came from the fact that for 490 years they had failed to let their farmland lie fallow one year out of every seven as God had commanded in **Leviticus 25:1-7**. The Lord had been patient all that time but finally had sent them to Babylon to give the land the 70 years of rest that were due it. (**2 Chron. 36:21**)

The beginning of **Daniel 9** documents Daniel's prayer, reminding the Lord that the 70 year time of punishment was nearly over and asking for mercy on behalf of his people. Before he could finish his prayer, the angel Gabriel appeared to him and spoke the words that we know as

Daniel 9:24-27. Let's read the whole thing to get the overview and then take it apart verse by verse.

Seventy weeks are determined upon your people and your Holy City to finish transgression, to put an end to sin, to atone for wickedness, to bring in everlasting righteousness, to seal up vision and prophecy and to anoint the most Holy. Know and understand this: From the issuing of the decree to restore and rebuild Jerusalem until The Anointed One the Ruler comes there will be seven weeks and sixty two weeks. It will be rebuilt with streets and a trench but in times of trouble. After the sixty two weeks the Anointed One will be cut off and have nothing. The people of the ruler who will come will destroy the city and the sanctuary. The end will come like a flood: War will continue till the end and desolations have been decreed. He will confirm a covenant with many for one week. In the middle of the week he will put an end to sacrifice and offering. And on a wing of the Temple he will set up an abomination that causes desolation until the end that is decreed is poured out on him (**Daniel 9:24-27**).

No prophecy in all of Scripture is more critical to our understanding of the end times than these four verses. A few basic clarifications are in order first, then we'll interpret the passage verse by verse. The Hebrew word translated weeks (or sevens) refers to a period of 7 years, like the English word decade refers to a period of 10 years. It literally means "a week of years." So 70 weeks is 70 X 7 years or 490 years. This period is divided into three parts, 7 weeks or 49 years, 62 weeks or 434 years, and 1 week or 7 years. Let's begin.

Seventy weeks are determined upon your people and your Holy City to finish transgression, to put an end to sin, to atone for wickedness, to bring in everlasting righteousness, to seal up vision and prophecy and to anoint the most Holy (place) (**Daniel 9:24**).

Sitting upon His heavenly throne, God decreed that six things would be accomplished for Daniel's people (Israel) and Daniel's Holy City (Jerusalem) during a specified period of 490 years. (I've inserted the word "place" after Holy at the end of the verse to clarify the fact that it refers to the Jewish Temple in Jerusalem.)

We should be aware that in Hebrew these things read a little differently. Literally, God had determined to;

1. restrict or restrain the transgression (also translated rebellion)
2. seal up their sins (as if putting them away in a sealed container)
3. make atonement (restitution) for their iniquity
4. bring them into a state of everlasting righteousness
5. seal up (same word as #2) vision and prophecy
6. anoint (consecrate) the most Holy place (sanctuary)

In plain language, God would put an end to their rebellion against Him, put away their sins and pay the penalties they had accrued, bring the people into a state of perpetual righteousness, fulfill the remaining prophecies, and anoint the Temple. This was to be accomplished through their Messiah (Jesus) because no one else could do it. Had they accepted Him as their savior their rebellion against

God would have ended. Their sins would have all been forgiven, and the full penalty paid for them. They would have entered into a state of eternal righteousness, all their prophecies would have been fulfilled and the rebuilt temple would have been consecrated. It should be noted here that although it appears to have been accepted by Him, God never dwelt in the 2nd Temple, nor was the ark of the covenant and its mercy seat ever present therein.

Know and understand this: From the issuing of the decree to restore and rebuild Jerusalem until The Anointed One the Ruler comes there will be seven weeks and sixty two weeks. It will be rebuilt with streets and a trench but in times of trouble (**Daniel 9:25**).

Here is a clear prophecy of the timing of the First Coming. When this message was given to Daniel by the angel Gabriel, Jerusalem had lain in ruin for nearly 70 years and the Jews were captive in Babylon. Counting forward for 62 + 7 periods of 7 years each (a total of 483 years) from a future decree giving the Jews permission to restore and rebuild Jerusalem, they should expect the Messiah.

To avoid confusion, it's important to distinguish the decree that freed the Jews from their captivity from the one that gave them permission to rebuild Jerusalem.

When he conquered Babylon in 535BC Cyrus the Persian immediately freed the Jews. It had been prophesied 150 years earlier in **Isaiah 44:24-45:6** and was fulfilled in **Ezra 1:1-4**. But according to **Nehemiah 2:1** the decree to rebuild Jerusalem was given in the first month of the 20th year of his reign by King Artaxerxes of Persia (March of 445 BC on our calendar, about 90 years later). Exactly 483 years after that decree the Lord Jesus rode in to Jerusalem on a donkey to shouts of "Hosanna"! It was the only day in His life that He permitted His followers to proclaim Him as Israel's King, fulfilling Daniel's prophecy to the day! The Hebrew in **Daniel 9:25** calls Him Messiah the Prince, denoting the fact that He was coming as the Anointed Son of the King and was not yet crowned King Himself.

In **Luke 19:41-45**, Jesus reminded the people of the specific nature of this prophecy. As he approached Jerusalem and saw the city, he wept over it and said, "*If you, even you, had only known on this day what would bring you peace—but now it is hidden from your eyes. The days will come upon you when your enemies will build an embankment against you and encircle you and hem you in on every side. They will dash you to the ground, you and the children within your walls. They will not leave one stone on another, because you did not recognize the time of God's coming to you.*" He held them accountable for knowing **Daniel 9:24-27**.

A few days later He extended that accountability to those who would be alive in Israel during the End Times. "*So when you see standing in the holy place 'the abomination that causes desolation,' spoken of through the prophet Daniel—let the reader understand— then let those who are in Judea flee to the mountains.* (**Matt 24:15-16**) They will also be required to understand **Daniel 9**.

After the sixty two weeks the Anointed One will be cut off and have nothing. The people of the ruler who will come will destroy the city and the sanctuary. The end will come like a flood: War will continue till the end and desolations have been decreed (**Daniel 9:26**).

First came 7 sevens (49 years) and then 62 sevens (434 years) for a total of 69 sevens or 483 years. The Hebrew word for Anointed One is Mashaich (Messiah in English). At the end of this 2nd period their Messiah would be cut off, which means to be executed or literally destroyed in the making of a covenant, having received none of the honor, glory and blessing the Scriptures promised Him.

Make no mistake about it. Jesus had to die so these 6 promises could come true. No one else in Heaven or on Earth could accomplish this. We can only imagine how different things would have been if they had accepted Him as their Messiah and let Him die for their sins so He could bring them into everlasting righteousness with His resurrection. But of course God knew they wouldn't, so He had to do things the hard way.

Do you realize what that means? It wasn't killing the Messiah that put the Jews at odds with God. After all He came to die for them. No. It's that in killing Him, they refused to let His death pay for their sins so He could save them. This had the effect of making His death meaningless to them. That's what severed the relationship.

Because of that, we now get the first hint that all would not go well. Following the crucifixion the people of a ruler yet to come would destroy Jerusalem and the Temple, the same Temple that God decreed would be consecrated. The Israelites would be scattered abroad and peace would elude the world.

We all know that Jesus was crucified and 38 years later the Romans put the torch to the city and the Temple destroying both. Surviving Jews were forced to flee for their lives and in the ensuing 2000 years I don't believe a single generation has escaped involvement in a war of some kind.

After the crucifixion something strange happened: The Heavenly clock stopped. 69 of the 70 weeks had passed and all that was prophesied to happen during those 483 years had come to pass but there was still one week (7 years) left. There are hints in the Old Testament that the clock had stopped several times before in Israel's history when for one reason or another they were either under subjugation or out of the land. And in the New Testament we're also given hints that while God is dealing with the Church, time ceases to exist for Israel (**Acts 15:13-18**). But the clearest indication of the stopped clock is that the events foretold in **Daniel 9:27** simply haven't happened yet.

He will confirm a covenant with many for one week. In the middle of the week he will put an end to sacrifice and offering. And on a wing of the Temple he will set up an abomination that causes desolation until the end that is decreed is poured out on him.

It's vital to our understanding of the End Times that we realize two things here. First, the Age of Grace didn't follow the Age of Law, it merely interrupted the Age of Law seven years short of its promised duration. These seven years have to be completed for God to accomplish the six things the angel listed in verse 24 for Israel.

And second, the Age of Grace was not the next step in the progression of God's overall plan, but was a deviation from it. Once the rapture comes, nothing like the Age of Grace will ever happen again (**Ephes. 2:6-7**). Even when Israel accepts the New Covenant, as **Jeremiah 31:31-34** promises, they won't enjoy the same benefits the Church has enjoyed. The relationship the Church has with the Lord will never be repeated with any other group. Ever.

But before we try to understand the 70th week let's review a rule of grammar that will help make our interpretation correct. The rule is this: Pronouns refer us back to the closest previous noun. Therefore the personal pronoun "He" in **Daniel 9:27** has to refer to the closest previous personal noun, in this case the "ruler who will come." So a ruler who will come from the territory of the old Roman Empire will confirm a 7 year covenant with Israel that permits them to build a Temple and re-instate their Old Covenant worship system. 3 1/2 years later he will violate the covenant by setting up an abomination that causes the Temple to become desolate, putting an end to their worship. This abomination brings the wrath of God down upon him and he will be destroyed.

The most obvious way in which we know these things haven't happened is that the Jewish Old Covenant worship system requires a Temple and there hasn't been one since 70 AD when the Romans destroyed it.

Some say this prophecy was fulfilled during the Roman destruction but most believe it's yet future, partly because of the term Abomination that causes Desolation. It's a specific insult to God that has happened only once previously. Antiochus Epiphanes, a powerful Syrian king, had attacked Jerusalem and entered the Temple area in 168BC. There he had sacrificed a pig on the Temple altar and erected a statue of the Greek god Zeus with his own face on it. He then required everyone to worship it on pain of death. This rendered the Temple unfit for worshiping God and so incensed the Jews that they revolted and defeated the Syrians. This is all recorded in Jewish history (1st Maccabees) where it's called the Abomination of Desolation. The subsequent cleansing of the Temple is celebrated to this day in the Feast of Hanukkah.

Paul warned us that in the latter days a world leader will become so powerful that he will exalt himself above everything that is called god or is worshiped and will stand in the Temple proclaiming himself to be God (**2 Thes 2:4**). In **Rev 13:14-15** we're told that he'll have a statue of himself erected and require everyone to worship it on pain of death. In **Matt 24:15-21** Jesus said that the Abomination that causes Desolation spoken of by Daniel will kick off the Great Tribulation, a period of time 3 1/2 years long that coincides with the last half of Daniel's 70th week. The similarities between this coming event and the one from history being so obvious, most scholars are persuaded that one points to the other since nothing in the intervening years fits so completely.

Soon And Very Soon

A new leader will soon emerge on the scene, a man with great personal charisma. Following a devastating war in the Middle East he'll present a plan to restore peace, by which he will quickly captivate and control the world. Since all true believers will have recently disappeared from Earth in the rapture of the Church, he'll have no trouble persuading most remaining inhabitants that he is the promised Messiah, the Prince of Peace. He will astound and amaze them all with feats of diplomacy and conquest, even performing the supernatural.

When he claims to be God, all hell will break loose on Earth and 3 1/2 years of the most terrible times mankind has ever known will threaten their very existence. But before they're all destroyed the real Prince of Peace will return and overthrow this impostor. He will set up His kingdom on earth, a kingdom that will never be destroyed or left to another.

Having given His life to finish transgression, put an end to sin, atone for wickedness and bring in everlasting righteousness, and having fulfilled all Biblical vision and prophecy, He will anoint the most Holy Place and receive all the honor, glory and blessing the Scriptures promise Him. Israel will finally have her Kingdom back and will live in peace with God in her midst forever. You can almost hear the footsteps of the Messiah.